LOSE CONTROL

The Way to Find Your Soul

MARY SHANNON HOFFPAUIR

Abingdon Women

Nashville

Lose Control
The Way to Find Your Soul

Copyright © 2020 Abingdon Press
All rights reserved.

ISBN-13: 978-1-7910-0435-4

20 21 22 23 24 25 26 27 28 29 — 10 9 8 7 6 5 4 3 2 1
MANUFACTURED IN THE UNITED STATES OF AMERICA

Contents

About the Author

Mary Shannon is a powerful and seasoned Bible teacher, author, and speaker whose great love for Jesus and Scripture inspires her audiences to "get their face in the Book!" Her background is rich with a spiritual upbringing rooted solidly in the Bible. But as a self-professed recovering perfectionist, she was bound by performance-based theology much of her Christian life, believing God's affection and approval were contingent on toeing the line of legalism—on measuring up. Most comfortable in a ball cap and ripped jeans, Mary Shannon is a gifted storyteller with a sassy sense of humor and a fresh transparency about the messiness of life: a recipe providing her with fresh insight and ample illustrations that are sure to make you laugh and cry as she brings the Bible to life for the ordinary person. After teaching the Bible in the classroom for many years, she began to teach women in her community; and today she leads three large community women's Bible study groups in the Phoenix metropolitan area (200–300 women each), as well as teaches across the nation as a featured speaker with the Aspire Women's Events. The loves of her life are her daughter, Hillary, and her late son, Zach (1994–2020).

Follow Mary Shannon:

 @ itsmaryshannon

 @ itsmaryshannon

Video messages/blog   itsmaryshannon.com
(check here also for event dates and booking information)

Preface

I have spent years of my life grappling for control, trying to orchestrate my life to fulfill my dreams and desires. Appearing to have it all together as a Christian, wife, mother, teacher, church member, and friend left me exhausted and at the end of my rope. To be honest, I was an anxiety-ridden mess, though I tried to keep that on the down low for years. My greatest fear was losing control, which would signify failure and expose the façade I portrayed to those around me. I kept people at arm's length for fear they would see the real me, which was struggling to keep it together. I knew this was not Christ's desire for me, yet I continued to repeat the same patterns. Have you ever wondered, *How can I give God complete control of my life? How can I live abundantly?*

That is where I was in my life when I heard the news that Mary Shannon (whom I call Shannon) had tragically lost her amazing son, Zachary. As a mom, it truly was my worst nightmare, the ultimate loss of control. Watching my friend, who loves Jesus with all her heart, struggling to keep moving forward was heartbreaking. Having breakfast together two weeks after Zach's passing, Shannon asked me if I would read this Bible study, *Lose Control: The Way to Find Your Soul*. As I dove into the study, I quickly recognized patterns in my life that were just like the Israelites. I wanted things to go my way, yet I ignored the "Samuels" God had placed in my path. My desire to be in control of my life was causing me to push away the King of my heart, much the same as the Israelites did. I began to wonder, *Will I trust God even when painful things happen? Will I be willing to believe that His ways are better than mine?*

As I continued the study, Saul became king, and things didn't go so well. Was God still in control then? Did Saul's mistakes, like my mistakes, ultimately ruin God's work? Absolutely not. As we see throughout the Scriptures, God uses all things to fulfill His purposes. Even though the Israelites insisted on their way, King David's succession paved the way for our Savior. Guided through these chapters in the Old Testament, I recognized that the mistakes and patterns I had developed to feel in control were meaningless, and that nothing could thwart the plans of God!

As I studied, I recognized how much I was learning and how much this study will help other women. Yet I also was in awe of God's providence. The words God gave Shannon as she wrote this study were not only meant to help us but also to help her through a time when everything in her life would completely spin out of control. As she began writing this study, she had no idea what she was about to experience. I texted Shannon to check on her one day, and she was so down. Her momma's heart was missing Zachary so much, and the pain was unbearable. That day I just happened to be reading these words from her study, which I texted back to her: God does not withhold Himself from you in times of trouble; He runs to you. Everything in Scripture was written to say, "Keep going, girl. Stick with it."

Regardless of the fortitude of your fears or your façade, this study will encourage and equip you to do just that—to keep going, trusting that you can lose control because He never does.

Laurie Bennett

Introduction

Have you ever thought you had your life under control—until you didn't? Perhaps you said things like "God is in control" or "God's got this," all the while living your life as if you're the one who has to hold it all together. It's like walking around with a cup of hot coffee, afraid it will spill with one wrong move. And when it does, making a mess, you realize what little control you actually have and how dependent on God you are.

I've known what that is like, which was the impetus for me writing this Bible study. But I never could have imagined that near the end of the writing process I would find myself in that place once again when my beloved son, Zachary, died suddenly and unexpectedly. Yes, I know what it is like to lose control and realize that the only way to find and hold onto your soul is to cling desperately to our God who is always in control.

Over the next six weeks, we will journey together through the Book of First Samuel, which tells an epic story about a fight for control. As we dig into the saga of Saul and David, Israel's first two kings, we will discover that no plan or purpose of God can be thwarted by human beings or by anything that happens to us. Even the worst of circumstances can be used by God to accomplish His purposes in our lives. I'm believing that with everything within me, friend, and you can too.

Getting Started

As we dive into the Book of First Samuel, we will study verse by verse until we reach the final chapters, which are not written in chronological order. Then we will maneuver through the story a little differently for better understanding. Each week there are five lessons combining study of Scripture with reflection and application. As part of the study content, you'll find a Scripture Focus and one or more Extra Insights in the margin, plus a daily Prayer Prompt that offers suggestions for talking with God about how you can apply what you're learning in your own life.

Space is provided for recording your responses and completing exercises as you read through each lesson. I encourage you to do this work not only so that you will be prepared for the discussion of the group session (if you are meeting with a group), but also so that you will get the most from this study that you possibly can. I've found in my own life that what I put into a Bible study determines what I will get from it.

Each daily lesson should take about twenty to thirty minutes to complete. You'll need a Bible, a pen, and an open heart that is ready to receive whatever God might have to teach you. Then as you gather with your group to watch the *Lose Control* DVD, you will have the opportunity to share what you are learning and pray together. (Streaming video files are available at www.Cokesbury.com, or you may access the video for this study and other Abingdon Women studies on AmplifyMedia.com through an individual or church membership.)

Each video message is designed to follow and complement the content that you have studied during the week. Whether or not your group watches the video, it's so helpful to share your struggles and victories in your journey to "lose control" and trust God with every aspect of your life. As you do, you'll encourage one another and find strength to complete the study and put into practice all that you're learning.

A Final Word

Friend, when our circumstances and our faith are shaken, that is when we can let go of our exhausted and futile attempts to pretend that we have it all together. That is when we realize we don't have control, and we never did. That is when we discover just how much we can trust our loving, sovereign God. And in this process of learning to surrender, that is when we find our soul—which is tethered to our unshakable, unfailing God. He loves you more than you can ever fully comprehend, and He longs to lead you into the freedom of a life surrendered completely to Him.

Mary Shannon

Biblical Background

First Samuel is a book that documents Israel's quest for a king. The problem is that they already had one: God. He had never let them down. From the first call of Abraham, God had committed Himself to Abraham's family, promising to guide and protect them, growing them into a great nation, and planting them in the land of Israel. The fruit of this nation would be the awaited Messiah. Their journey would be one of faith, which their founding father Abraham would demonstrate by waiting an entire lifetime to see one miraculous shoot, his son Isaac, bursting forth.

Over time and despite great oppression from the Egyptians, the nation grew. God chose Moses to lead His people to freedom, and at the base of Mt. Sinai they officially entered into a covenant relationship with God (their king). Under His instructions, they established a sacrificial system of worship and built a way of life based on laws promoting personal morality, social justice, and practical kindness. With all the foundations built, it was time for Moses to move this once-slave nation into their homeland, Israel.

Have you ever wondered why God placed His people in the land of Israel? I mean, come on! He could have put them anywhere in the world, and He chose to place them in this tiny narrow piece of land that is only 85 miles wide and 290 miles long.[1] It's approximately the size of the state of New Jersey.[2] This land contained one of the greatest trade routes in the world, called "The Way of the Sea" or The Via Maris. It connected the world at the time, linking all of Egypt with the land of Mesopotamia.[3]

God placed His people right in the crossroads of life so the world would be able to see this peculiar group of people who worshiped a living God, not a god carved out of wood or stone. Yet, instead of ridding the land of its current inhabitants as God had instructed them to do, the Israelites settled among the native people. Instead of the nation of Israel influencing the world through their way of life, the world began to influence them. They traded their newfound freedom for a new brand of bondage.

You see, at Sinai the nation of Israel had entered into a covenant with God. This covenant was much like a marriage covenant, so the language should sound very familiar to us. They were to love and remain faithful to Him alone. They were to honor His name because they were commissioned to represent His name to the nations. He designated one day away from the normal distractions of work to focus only on their relationship with Him.

The nation agreed to all God had said through Moses and entered into this conditional covenant, which included blessings and curses. This makes sense to me, because if we live our lives loving God and others, it brings life to all. If not, it brings pain.

Years later, we encounter the Israelites living in their promised land, consistently being unfaithful to their God. They have habitually fallen for the gods of others (cheating on their loving God), and when they do, God removes His hedge of protection and oppression comes from all sides from pagan nations—the Midianites, the Canaanites, the Perezites—and maybe even the mosquito bites!

Different nations. Different times. Oppressing in different ways. Every time the nation of Israel cries out to God for deliverance, He is faithful to raise up a judge to lead and deliver them. As long as the nation of Israel has a strong leader enforcing their worship of Yahweh and Him alone, they are obedient and they live in a time of peace. Yet, as soon as that judge dies, they return to their idolatry and the cycle continues. This cycle, which is represented in the graph below, consumes the nation of Israel for four hundred years!

How many times would the nation of Israel need to be reminded that God was in control and He could be trusted? When would they stop acting like "the horse or the mule, which have no understanding but must be controlled by bit and bridle" (Psalm 32:9 NIV)?

Well, this will be the ongoing lesson in the book of 1 Samuel. Instead of realizing their true problem, their lack of trust, *the people of Israel decide* the solution is a king. Just another "bit and bridle." They want to be like all the other nations. The problem is they are already like the other nations and they don't even recognize it. They are treating the God who has called them, formed them, and delivered them as if He were made of wood or stone.

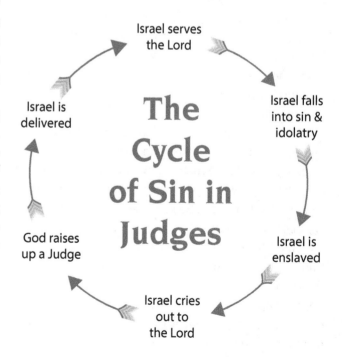

The Cycle of Sin in Judges

Israel serves the Lord

Israel falls into sin & idolatry

Israel is enslaved

Israel cries out to the Lord

God raises up a Judge

Israel is delivered

Week 1

I Believe God Is in Control

Giving Lip Service Without Heart Commitment

1 Samuel 1–6

DAY 1

The Book of 1 Samuel begins with the story of Hannah, which we will explore in our video teaching this week. As we will see, Hannah, who was barren, was a godly woman and, therefore, an *exception* among the people of her time. But today we begin our study by taking a good look at a few other characters who represent the *norm* of the day—the high priest Eli and his sons Hophni and Phinehas. If Hannah was the light, Eli was the twilight and Hophni and Phinehas were the darkness. Yet, just as Hannah's barrenness did not prove God uncaring or out of control, neither should we assume that Eli's lack of discernment or his sons' wickedness was out of the notice and ultimate control, or sovereignty, of a loving God. Sometimes it's hard to see God in the darkness, but He is there and always at work. God never loses control.

Read 1 Samuel 1:9-14. Where did Eli usually sit? What did he assume about Hannah?

Eli's seat at the door of the temple was actually more like a throne. It was high and raised up.[1] His duty was to oversee all that went on in the Tabernacle. Yet what discernment did he really have?

Eli watched Hannah bring her heavy heart, her pain, and her hopelessness to God. He watched her pour out her broken heart before God, and he assumed she was drunk. Why did the guardian of worship not recognize Hannah's humility and sorrow?

I believe one reason is that this act of true worship was so rare in the days of the judges. Remember, these times were described as a time when "everyone did what was right in his own eyes" (Judges 21:25). That's a recipe for chaos.

The only thing that kept Israel in line during the time of the judges was a strong human leader. When a leader was committed to serving the Lord, the people were required to get rid of pagan worship and worship only Yahweh. Yet when that judge died, the people would once again worship pagan gods. I believe the nation of Israel during that time is a prime example of religious reformation, as opposed to spiritual revival.

> Religious reformation is a temporary change in behavior due to religious constraints.
> Spiritual revival is a permanent change of the heart.

I can't help but apply this to parenting. How often did I parent to see change in behavior yet fail to actually see change in the heart? How many times did I discipline behaviors only, without taking the time to investigate, understand, and teach the hearts of my children? Listen, I'm not telling you to reason with a three-year-old in the grocery line. No, we are to establish healthy hierarchies and boundaries. But many times, I was quick to rebuke as they got older because I believed their behaviors were a reflection of me and my parenting—and Lord knows I did not want people to think we weren't the perfect Christian family.

My adult son once told me that he wished parents would teach more like Jesus, using parables. Stories draw people in, allow listeners to come to their own conclusions, and continue to reveal deeper meanings. He said he wished I had been more transparent with him and told stories from my own life. I told him that I had lived in the fear that if I had shared my failures with him, he would have used them as permission to do the same. Yet, I understand now that this would have allowed me to teach truths through my humanity. By seeing my failures, he would have known perfection was never the standard in our home. We all need grace!

Eli was used to seeing people live their lives in obedience to a set of rules. They were going through the religious motions with no movement of the heart. Yet lowly Hannah, the exception to the norm, came in to pour out her heart to the Lord. The one who was "raised up" on his high seat or high horse failed to recognize not only true worship in another person, but also his own need for the same.

Eli knew the Lord, yet I wonder if over the years his relationship had become stale. Could this be because he was watching from an elevated view? How often do we as believers elevate ourselves above others, failing to see the plank in our own eyes?

Read 1 Samuel 2:12-17, and hold your place there. How does verse 12 describe Eli's sons?

Isn't it interesting that Eli is so quick to judge the heart of Hannah, yet he fails to judge his own sons? The one who was told she was worthless by her culture because she could not have children found her worth in the Lord. The one whom the culture elevated on his "throne" instead raised what the Bible calls "worthless" sons.

In your own words, how would you describe the connection between what 1 Samuel 2:12 says about Hophni and Phinehas and what 2 Timothy 3:5 (in the margin) says about people in the last days?

They will act religious, but they will reject the power that could make them godly. Stay away from people like that!
(2 Timothy 3:5 NLT)

—————

They'll make a show of religion, but behind the scenes they're animals. Stay clear of these people.
(2 Timothy 3:5 MSG)

The beginning of 1 Samuel 2:12 describes the sons of the high priest as "worthless." Where I am from, some might call them "good for nothin'." The second half of that same verse explains why: they did not know God! In other words, they had no personal relationship or intimate knowledge of God. They knew about Him, but they didn't *know* Him. Their father Eli had taught them the family business, yet they had no love for it. They had been taught to walk through the religious motions. This is so tricky! If I'm being honest, I often trained my kids how to live like a Christian instead of how to enjoy a vibrant relationship with Christ.

Extra Insight

The word "worthless" is *beliya'al* in Hebrew. It means "wicked" or "vile." It can also mean "unprofitable" or "of no fruit."[2]

Look again at 1 Samuel 2:12-17 and 22, and describe in your own words the behaviors we see in these sons.

With many of the offerings brought to the temple, a portion was given to God, a portion was given to the priests, and a portion was kept by the giver. Leviticus 10 tells us the portion given to the priests was to be the thigh and the breast. Yet Hophni and Phinehas decided to invite themselves into everyone's supper, and even before grace could be said, they sunk their fork into the roasting pot and did the ole dine and dash. They took whatever portion they wanted. If that was not bad enough, they also stole from God by taking their portion before the fat was burned off.

Not only did they take advantage of the people by stealing their offering, but they also took advantage of the young women who came to serve at the tabernacle, viewing God's offering and God's people as mere objects for their own gratification.

Hophni and Phinehas used the power of the priesthood to intimidate and manipulate people for their own benefit, and it did not take long for the people to no longer want to come and bring their offerings. The priests were to be the mediators between God and people, but instead of keeping the bridge open between the two, they created barriers. They themselves became true blockades to worship.

But you are not like that, for you are a chosen people. You are royal priests, a holy nation, God's very own possession. As a result, you can show others the goodness of God, for he called you out of the darkness into his wonderful light.

(1 Peter 2:9 NLT)

Journal your thoughts as you compare this Old Testament narrative with 1 Peter 2:9 (in the margin). What are the privileges and dangers of being a royal priesthood? In what ways might we as Christians or the church have been blockades to the world knowing the goodness of God?

Now read 1 Samuel 2:22-26. How old was Eli at this time?

As much as we would like to, we cannot go back and change the past. All we can do is make the right choice today.

The Scripture says that Eli was "very old," which suggests that these were not young men sowing their oats but grown men making a mockery of the priesthood and the tabernacle, waiting for Pops to kick the bucket so they could take over.

When you are old, it can be hard to look back and see that the fruit of your labor is rotten. How many hours had Eli spent wondering what he had done wrong? Was guilt now keeping him from handling the current situation? Actually, none of that matters because as much as we would like to, we cannot go back and change the past, so why waste time dwelling on it? All we can do is make the right choice today.

This is easier said than done. I know this firsthand. After my divorce, I found myself living alone with my two adult children. Now, let's be clear. I was *not* a perfect parent. My ex-husband and I wrestled to be on the same page in regards to discipline. I did my best to correct behavior, but when there is a lack of unity, every kid will find it and exploit it, including my own. Now I was alone with them, healing from a devastating divorce and trying to become all that God wanted me to be. Part of that meant becoming queen of my own castle. When adult kids experience the pain of divorce, they feel like their entire foundation has crumbled and wonder if all they knew was a lie. We were three hurting people living in one household. Yet somehow in the midst of all the pain and guilt, it was still my job to produce two adults who could stand on their own two feet, treating me and others with love and respect.

So, without sharing the gory details, just know I established boundaries and held to them. Now believe me, when you change your dance moves, everyone who is used to dancing with you will freak out! It was rough for a while, but I knew that healthy boundaries were the best thing for all parties, so I stayed consistent. They began to realize that if they chose to dance with me, these were the moves. We began to hear music that sounded more like love and respect than screaming.

Eli had many opportunities to address the behaviors of his sons. When the Scripture says that he "heard all that his sons were doing" (v. 22 NASB), the idea in the Hebrew is that he "kept hearing" or "heard from time to time."[3] This was not new information. These boys had been doing these things for some time, yet Eli failed to discipline them—not only as their father but also as their boss, the high priest. The true consequence for their behaviors was death.

The repercussions for Hophni and Phinehas's actions would come later. For now, Eli just talked. He was still trying to reason with men who had lost all sense of reason, men who needed to repent but instead were scorning the offerings of God. If Eli had not previously sown the seed of respect in his sons, he was not going to reap it now. Therefore, they ignored the words of their father because, frankly, talk is cheap.

Read 1 Samuel 2:27-36, and finish the story in your own words below. What did the prophet say to Eli in regards to his sons? What would happen to them?

What specifically would happen to Eli's descendants?

Why do you think the prophet spoke to Eli as if he were the one who had scorned the offerings? (v. 29)

Friend, God wants what every good parent wants: true relationship. He wants you and not an ornery mule "that needs a bit and bridle to stay on track" (Psalm 32:9 MSG). If all you're doing is walking through the religious motions, stop! You are on a road to nowhere. God wants your heart, because from it flows your authentic self.

Prayer Prompt

Spend some time with your Father today. Be honest about your feelings, your situations, your screw-ups, and your regrets. Allow the Father's love to become both a healing salve to your wounds and a sweet melody for some new dance moves!

DAY 2

Scripture Focus

1 Samuel 2:18-21; 3:1-14

Yesterday our focus was on the high priest Eli and his two scoundrel sons Hophni and Phinehas, who were a representation of the rest of the nation of Israel, a people walking through the motions of religion but having no true heart for God. Yet, the author places a small section of Scripture in the middle of this chapter that proves to be an exercise in contrast, shining the light on a young boy named Samuel—Hannah's son. He will show us that God is in control; and if the priesthood won't listen to Him, then He will raise up someone who will.

Read 1 Samuel 2:18-21. Where did Samuel grow up?

In the middle of the darkness of chapter 2, we meet this young boy clothed in a white linen ephod, the official dress of the priests. Can't you see the light of hope jumping off the page of Scripture? Can't you just sense the innocence? Samuel had been dedicated to the Lord by his mother as a fulfillment of an oath she made to God for giving her a son.

Take a look at 1 Samuel 3:1. According to this verse, what did Samuel do in the temple?

God does not value the motions as much as the motivations.

I love how one Bible version describes it: he was "ministering to the Lᴏʀᴅ" (ESV). This young boy was doing what would have been considered menial or simple tasks, yet these tasks were performed out of a pure heart. I'm sure the tasks of Hophni and Phinehas seemed much more important, but we know that God does not value the motions as much as the motivations. This young boy honestly was the closest thing the people of Israel had to a true minister.

Are you a minister according to the definition in the margin? In what ways do you minister? To whom do you minister?

Extra Insight

Minister (verb)—to give service, care, or aid; attend, as to wants or necessities; to contribute, as to comfort or happiness.[4]

Often we forget that we all are called to minister to those around us, and sometimes those in official ministry forget that their position is not one of power or prestige but of service. Even Jesus took the form, or nature, of a servant (see Philippians 2:5-11).

First Samuel 2:19 tells us that Hannah made her son a robe every year and brought it to him when she and her husband, Elkanah, would come for the annual sacrifice. I can just picture her sitting by candlelight after all her chores were done and sewing this robe as she thought and prayed for her little boy. He was living proof that God had heard her prayers and cared for her. If God had brought Samuel to her, then she would trust that God would lead, guide, and protect him in her absence.

It could not have been easy for Samuel to grow up in an environment with Hophni and Phinehas. Most of us parents, especially when our kids are young, want to isolate them from the influences of jokers like these two. And yet here Hannah dropped off her kid to live with them, growing up in the shadow and under the bad influence of these privileged scalawags. It almost seems like the male version of Cinderella and her two wicked stepsisters. Maybe this is the point. Had Eli created an environment of image, prestige, and ease that promoted an attitude of entitlement in his sons?

How can we expect to grow or mature if we never experience hardship? We need to stop asking God to get us out of every hard situation and start asking Him *what* we can get out of this hard situation. Jesus did not avoid suffering. In fact, Hebrews 5:8 (NIV) says, "He learned obedience from what he suffered." He suffered on a cross so you and I could experience salvation and new life. Jesus was very clear that in order to follow Him, we too must carry crosses (Matthew 16:24). We too will suffer!

Sometimes in our suffering we feel that God is silent. Did you notice that 1 Samuel 3:1 says "the word of the Lord was rare in those days"? Why would God choose to be silent? Didn't He care about His people?

Have you ever given advice over and over to someone you love just to watch them ignore it? Eventually, we stop giving it because they haven't listened to the advice we have already given them. God's people were experiencing what Amos 8:11 calls a famine "of hearing the words of the Lord." They had no appetite for God's Word, so He took away even the opportunity to hear it.

God promised that if we seek Him with all of our hearts, we will find Him (Jeremiah 29:13), but doesn't it often seem as if He is purposefully hiding from us? It could be that He has already shown us many things that we are ignoring, and He is patiently waiting for us to address those.

I remember watching my child have a fit while I patiently waited for him or her to stop and obey my instructions. How ironic that when the word of the Lord was rare, God spoke to a child.

Read 1 Samuel 3:2-10, and hold your place there. Do you believe the description of Eli's eyesight is only literal, or could it also have some spiritual significance? Explain.

Extra Insight

The Hebrew verb for "grow dim" in 1 Samuel 3:2, *keheh*,[5] comes from the same root verb used in 3:13 for "to restrain."[6] Perhaps the narrator is drawing our attention to the key reason why Eli's vision was dimmed, because he failed to restrain his sons.

What things had Eli overlooked? Write your insights below.

Where does this Scripture say Samuel was lying down?

The author is painting a beautiful picture with a word play on darkness and light. Here you have Eli lying down in his "usual" place, a place of routine. Just as his eyes had become dim from old age, his spiritual vision had become dull as well. He chose not to see the behaviors of his sons and their effect on the people. He failed to see the true humility of Hannah and his own need for repentance. Here he lay in his dimly lit room while the young, bright-eyed Samuel lay in the Tabernacle.

The author tells us that the lamp of God had not gone out yet. This refers to the beautiful golden lampstand located in the Tabernacle tent within the first room known as the Holy Place. It stood at the left side of the Holy Place.[7] The Table of Presence would have been on the right side,[8] leaving the altar of incense front and center before the veil that separated the Holy Place from the Holy of Holies.[9] In this sacred place, this young boy slept at the base of the flaming candelabra, probably still dressed in his little white ephod. Samuel had fallen asleep as close to the presence of God as he was allowed, possibly waiting for the lamps to dim so he could fill the oil that was never to run out. Just another menial task, right?

I can just see the Father's smile as he looked down on this innocent boy bathed in the symbolic light of His Spirit, knowing that tonight Samuel would become a true prophet in Israel. Tonight young Samuel would hear the voice of God.

Write in your own words the sequence of events that occur in verses 4-10.

Extra Insight

Look up Genesis 22:1, Genesis 46:2, Exodus 3:4, Isaiah 6:8, and Acts 9:10 for other instances when God called individuals by name and they responded with "Here I am."

How sweet that each time Samuel heard his name being called, he went to Eli. This shows not only his willingness to serve but also his respect for and obedience to Eli. He seemed to be able to go right into Eli's room when called, so we might assume true parental informality and affection. Could Eli have become like a grandparent raising a grandson, hoping for a second chance at parental redemption? Once again, though, we see the "dim eyes" of Eli as it took him three chances to finally recognize what was going on. We can't judge Samuel for naivety, because Scripture tells us that Samuel "did not yet know the Lord; and the word of the Lord had not yet been revealed to him" (1 Samuel 3:7). Literally, the Hebrew term *yada'* suggests that Samuel was not acquainted with nor hadn't heard from the Lord.[10]

Had Eli only taught Samuel how to perform the works of the Tabernacle yet failed to teach him about the God of the Tabernacle? Or did Eli simply not have any personal experience with God Himself? Possibly both. But the story tells us that when Eli realized God was speaking to young Samuel, he did teach Samuel what to do.

I love Eli's instructions. He told Samuel to go back to where he had been, lie down, and wait. Now that is amazing advice. How often do we quiet ourselves and make ourselves available to hear God? Our world is so busy! There is so much noise, activity, and distraction that I wonder if we are even able to hear when God is trying to speak to us.

This is why I go to the mountain trails daily to run and talk with God. It is my time to get away from distraction. Sometimes I'm quiet; sometimes I scream it out, cry it out, or if I'm honest, cuss it out. But every day we hash it out. I know one thing: if you run a long enough distance, you finally come to the end of yourself—left with the energy only to listen, to "be still, and know that I am God" (Psalm 46:10).

According to 1 Samuel 3:11-14, what message did Samuel receive?

What did Samuel do after he had received this message? (v. 15)

If you received a message from God to give to a spiritual leader (especially a negative one like this), or even a person of any powerful position, wouldn't you have a hard time sleeping? When Eli came to Samuel the next morning, he instructed Samuel not to leave out a single word. Samuel did not! This is the sign of a true prophet: obedience.

How amazing that in the presence of the priesthood God chose to speak to and through a child. Could it be because he was the only one with ears to hear and a heart to obey—the only one who was willing to open the door? Oh, the beauty of childlike faith! The bright eyes of expectancy not yet clouded by the disappointments of this world. Authenticity not yet shrouded by layers of protection. May we be like young Samuel, more aware of being loved than being imperfect.

Extra Insights

Eli recognized that God was trying to speak to this young boy personally. Often as parents or mentors, we feel the pressure of bringing God's word or wisdom to children when God is capable of doing that Himself. Let's show our kids how to go to a quiet place to wait and listen for God to speak and, when He does, to respond with "here I am."

———

Eli told Samuel to respond if God spoke. Our posture of waiting and listening will not always produce a voice. We wait with expectation, but we do not presume.

Prayer Prompt

Run into your Father's "room" today! The door is always open. Shout, "Here I am!" Ask your Father to reveal the areas of your life where your eyes have become dim. Ask Him to pour His love over you. Now, let that child inside you drink it in, because God's love will produce the trust necessary for you to climb out of any ditch, dark place, or difficult situation.

DAY 3

Yesterday, the end of 1 Samuel 3 left us with the hope for Israel's future under the reliable leadership of Samuel as their priest, prophet, and judge. Yet as we begin chapter 4 today, we are reminded that the present stability of the nation is anything but reliable.

Once again Israel would battle with a neighboring people for land rights. The Philistines were no joke. These Aegean people, most likely from the island of Crete, had made their way to the land of Israel hundreds of years before. They had already settled along the Mediterranean coast by the time the Israelites made their exodus out of Egypt. They were more advanced than the Israelites, with their innovative use of iron and their aggressive military policies.[11] Like most of the surrounding nations, they were polytheistic, which means they worshiped many gods. But as the story will reveal, Dagon was their chief god.

Read 1 Samuel 4:1-4.

How many Israelites died on the battlefield that day (v. 2)?

How did the elders decide to proceed in hopes of turning the tide of the battle (v. 3)?

The ark played center stage in the battle at Jericho, which we read about in Joshua 6. This was the first battle the Israelites faced when taking the Promised Land under the leadership of Joshua. Jericho was a stronghold city that connected the two dominant trade routes in the land of Israel. It was highly fortified and well defended; but if the Israelites were going to conquer the land of Israel, they had to conquer Jericho.

The Book of Joshua tells us that the angel of the Lord, with his drawn sword, had shown himself to Joshua one day as Joshua was scouting Jericho. Joshua, being a smart guy, asked him, "Whose side are you on?" Not a bad question when you are facing a man with a drawn sword. In present day vernacular, the angel responded, "I'm not here to take sides. I'm here to take over." He then laid out the battle plan before Joshua: Walk around the city once a day for six days, but on the seventh day walk around seven times, ending with a loud battle cry. You may know what happened—and if you don't, be sure and read Joshua chapter 6. As the children's song says, "The walls came a tumbling down," and Jericho was defeated.

What interests me in relation to our story in 1 Samuel is the formation the angel told the Israelites to get into as they walked around the walls.

Read Joshua 6:8-12. What was the order of procession? List it below.

Extra Insight

A shofar is one of the earliest known musical instruments.[12] Made from a hollow ram's horn, the shofar was used both in battle (Job 39:25) and in liturgical celebrations (2 Samuel 6:15; Psalm 81:3).

Picture the Israelites approaching the walls of Jericho—the armed guards leading the way, followed by the seven priests blowing seven shofars (see Extra Insight) to announce the coming of the king, and a second group of armed guards following the ark of the covenant. The ark, lifted high on the priests' shoulders, symbolized the king's throne. The people of God brought up the rear—approximately two million of them if the women and children were present. There are so many miracles in this story, one of which is keeping this many people silent as they walked around the approximate half-mile circumference of Jericho, especially if you assume the presence of women and children. Now that's funny! After all, this was a *king's* procession.

The point here is that the battle of Jericho was God's to fight. This was His plan, and all He asked of the Israelites was to follow. God told Joshua that He had already delivered Jericho into his hands (Joshua 6:2). The victory would be His.

Returning to our story in 1 Samuel 4, we might assume the elders are considering battles such as Jericho because they have come to the conclusion that they are losing since the ark of God is not present. The problem is that they have missed the whole point of Jericho. In the battle of Jericho, the ark represented the seat or throne of God, their king. This is because in the Tabernacle, the Shekinah glory of God lived above the mercy seat of the ark. The ark was a visual representation that God Himself was leading His people into battle according to His battle plan. They were showing their trust in Him by obediently following His plan. By the way, nothing about His plan would have seemed right to any human being, which reminds me of a couple of proverbs (take a look in the margin).

How could a plan so simple be so powerful? How could a plan of walking around a city for seven days work? Couldn't we also say this about God's plan of salvation? The idea of salvation by faith alone, without works, has baffled many for centuries. Some call this "easy believeism," but is it? Is it ever easy to truly trust God?

In this current battle with the Philistines in 1 Samuel 4:1-4, we do not see the Israelite people request, receive, or follow a plan from God, their king. Why? They had no true shepherd guiding them. They weren't experiencing a deep personal connection with God, and when they prayed, they heard nothing but silence. They were left walking through the motions of life based on ancient teachings, battling whatever came their way with whatever means possible. But this battle had gotten the best of them! This confrontation caused them to run for cover and reevaluate what they were doing. They knew this battle could not be won without the supernatural power of God. This battle was out of their control. It took a great defeat for the people to remember the God of the Exodus, the God of miracles.

I see the same tendency in myself. Why is God an afterthought for me so often? I wouldn't say it outright, but my lifestyle betrays that often I live as if I truly don't need Him. I can handle my day-to-day operations because I totally know how to live this Christian-life-thing. I know how to walk the walk. I know how to obey the rules (at least the big ones). That is, until the wheels fall off. Then I shake the dirt off, try to stop the bleeding, gather my senses, and ask, "What the heck just happened?" And I am left with a broken "box" that God has vacated—if He was ever in it to begin with. Because of my legalistic religious background, my first response tends to be that God is punishing me. Somehow I have left Him out of my life or haven't walked in His ways, and as a result "this is what I get." So out of fear, I run back and grab the Scriptures or go to church because if I can appease God, I will once again have victory—or more honestly, I can re-enter my comfort zone. Truth be known, the Scriptures, the sermons, and the encouraging social media posts come up short. Somewhere there is a disconnect.

There is a way that appears to be right,
  but in the end it leads to death.
    (Proverbs 14:12 NIV)

———

Many are the plans in a person's heart,
  but it is the Lord's purpose that prevails.
    (Proverbs 19:21 NIV)

Have you ever experienced a disconnect between your circumstances and what you believe about God? If so, write about it briefly.

Many pagan polytheistic people, like the Philistines, would bring offerings to appease their gods, who always seemed to be angry. They would actually carry images of their gods with them as they went to war to bring them good luck and victory, perhaps because victory might prove their god was stronger.[13]

The Israelites might have been lifting up the one true God in some way, but they were doing it like the pagans by making Him an image to be carried in and out of battle. The ark of the covenant had become a graven image representing God instead of a mercy seat upon which the living God would sit, dwell, and rule over His people. Yes, they ran back and grabbed His seat, but they left Him behind, so to speak.

How often do we treat the living God as a graven image to be carried around wherever we need Him? What are some ways that we, like the Israelites, put God in a box?

Finish reading 1 Samuel 4, verses 5-22.

Why do you think the people shouted when the ark entered the camp?

Do you think the people presumed that presence of the ark meant the presence of God?

Can we judge the presence of the Spirit by the noise in the sanctuary? Explain your response.

How interesting it is that we so often limit God. Wasn't this the very thing God had warned about in His second commandment (Exodus 20:4), essentially saying, "Do not attempt to confine me in an image. Remember, you were made in my image. I am not made in yours." Here the Israelites did what we all tend to do. They confined God to a box—something they could see, touch, and control. The ark in many ways represented God, but the ark was not God—nor was it a slam-dunk guarantee of success!

The Bible reveals God to us, yet the Bible is not God. God is the *living* Word. Sometimes I wonder if we wield the Bible much like the Israelites wielded the ark, carrying it into battle presuming our interpretations are right. Do we intimidate others to instill fear in our enemies? Do we believe that if we give it priority, we won't have defeat? The Bible leads us to God, but it too cannot contain Him. Even if we search it from cover to cover, there will always be places of mystery. Our God is alive!

In some ways, the Philistines had more respect for the God of the Israelites than the Israelites. The ruckus in the Israelite camp got the Philistines' attention, but it was the reputation of God that truly brought them fear. The stories from Egypt were still top news, and the Philistines were fully aware of the power of Israel's God.

This story ends in defeat for the Israelites, and the ark of the covenant is stolen by the Philistines. How could that be? Why would God allow these pagan people to take His ark? Was He not as powerful as they thought? Was He not paying attention? Did He not care?

Going through tough times of defeat, suffering, and pain will make us question God. We question His character and motives. When things are bad enough, we even question His existence. (Even the psalmist does that in Psalm 13. Check it out.) What happens when the things you thought you knew about God are stolen? What happens when the life you are experiencing doesn't seem to fit the box you constructed with Scripture? What happens when you come up with more questions than answers?

The Bible leads us to God, but it too cannot contain Him. Even if we search it from cover to cover, there will always be places of mystery.

When have you felt stuck in the messy middle between questions and faith?

In my opinion, when our faith is shaken, we can really start to grow. That's when we come to God confessing our brokenness, when we ask Him to break down our images and replace them with His true self. That's when the disconnect transfigures into glorious true relationship! Sister, stop depending on what you think you know about God or what you've been told about Him, and spend time actually getting to know Him. He is alive and still speaking!

Prayer Prompt

Bring all your questions before God today. Tell Him about your "disconnect" and your frustrations. Ask Him to teach you and to show you His heart and character. Give Him permission to break down any false images of Him that you or your traditions have built. Start a new journey with Him today. Let God out of the box!

DAY 4

Scripture Focus

1 Samuel 5; 6:1-12

As we concluded 1 Samuel 4 yesterday, we read that the prophecy given to Samuel about the house of Eli had been set into motion. The two sons of Eli, Hophni and Phinehas, were killed on the battlefield. When word got back to Eli regarding his sons—and especially the loss of the ark—he fell from his "lifted" seat and broke his neck, killing him. If that's not dreary enough, Phinehas's wife had a son and saddled him with the name Ichabod (no, not the Headless Horseman), which means "The Glory has departed from Israel." Imagine growing up with that name!

Maybe the dreary ending of chapter 4 begs for the comedic relief offered by chapter 5. This story makes me laugh every time. So, go ahead and jump right in!

Read 1 Samuel 5 and hold your place there.

Can you picture it? The Philistines bring the ark of the covenant into their own city of Ashdod. I can just hear the shouts. I bet there was dancing in the streets. They had defeated the Israelites, and they thought they had taken their god. The God who destroyed Egypt had been defeated. Or had He?

The interesting thing about these polytheistic people is their unwillingness to offend any god. Therefore, if an image such as the ark was captured, they would just add it to their temple alongside their other images. They placed the ark at the feet of their chief god, Dagon. Of course, they believed Dagon was more powerful, as evidenced by their latest victory, but they found no reason to offend the God of Israel. As we read the story, though, it seems God was not equally as worried about offending them. Yahweh does not share His glory with another.

Look again at 1 Samuel 5:1-5. In the space below, draw a picture of what the Philistines discovered as they entered their temple the next two mornings.

Extra Insight

The same Hebrew word used in the root of the name Ichabod (1 Samuel 4:21), meaning "not glory," is translated in 1 Samuel 5:6 as "heavy."[14] The glory of the Lord had departed from the Israelites with the loss of the ark. In Ashdod, the glory of the Lord seemed heavy handed (pun intended!). Whether we long for or dread the glory of the Lord, we must confess it has weight.

Two mornings in a row, the Philistines not only had to put their god back together but also back on his throne. Here we see people once more maneuvering their gods.

How ironic that next Dagon lost his head and his hands. A graven image has neither will nor power. The power resided in the ones putting their god back together! Lord knows, if I have to put my god back together, I am in big trouble because I can barely keep up with my own head and hands. Amen?

According to 1 Samuel 5:6 and 6:4, what were the Philistines afflicted with?

Okay, let's first address the tumors. The King James Version of the Bible refers to these tumors as "emerods," which comes from a root word meaning "to swell." The Hebrew word literally means "mound."[15] The context has led historians and Bible commentators to conclude that they were occurrences of tumors, boils, or maybe even hemorrhoids. Whatever you want to call them doesn't matter to me. All I know is that I wouldn't want them! I don't want any kind of swelling mound anywhere on my body. With that said, I can't help but imagine how helpless you would be to defend your land if you were dealing with mounds of hemorrhoids. Sitting would be questionable. Fighting would be impossible. Could this be the first recorded "pain in the butt"?

Chapter 6 lets us know that the Philistines had also been struck with plagues involving rats. (Maybe the tumors were a result of these plagues? I don't know. This could be one of those chicken-or-egg questions.) What I do know is that the people of Ashdod wanted that ark gone. The rest of chapter 5 fills us in on the game of "hot potato" that the Philistines started to play. "I don't want it. Here, you take it!" They passed the ark through the Philistine cities along the coast of the Mediterranean Sea, each time producing the same results. Finally it came to the city of Ekron.

Read 1 Samuel 6:1-6. How did the Philistines decide to deal with the ark?

Finally, the big dogs (priests and diviners) got together to decide what they were going to do with this ark. It couldn't possibly be a coincidence that every time this ark entered a city, the people were struck with disease and plague. So, they decided to somehow send it back to the Israelites. I imagine someone piping up and saying something like, "We can't send it back empty. I mean come on. If this god is angry, he will want parting gifts, right? Plus, I hear the God of Israel is really into guilt offerings. I'm not sure what those are, but I've actually heard about an incident in the desert where they were being bitten by serpents and their god had them make a bronze image of a serpent and raise it up. They literally had to look at what was killing them. So how about we make golden images of the rats and tumors?"

Seriously, the Philistines felt the heavy hand of God on them and their land. They determined to give God His due glory and not to harden their hearts like the Egyptians had done before them. The stubborn heart of Pharaoh had hurt his people, his nation, and his family, yet in no way did it hinder God's plan for His people to leave Egypt and enter the Promised Land.

Isn't that how it all started? Wanting to be like God, having knowledge and control. In the Garden, the serpent of old convinced Eve that she could be like God by knowing good and evil. The problem is, differentiating between good and evil is only one aspect of God. Having the knowledge of good and evil without possessing the power to use that knowledge wisely actually leaves us feeling more human than deity. We realize that knowledge does not mean control. Actually, the more knowledgeable I become, the more out of control I often feel. To be honest, sometimes I just want to live with my head in the sand. Isn't this what Paul was saying in Romans 7:8-11 (NLT)?

*8But sin used this command to arouse all kinds of covetous desires within me!
If there were no law, sin would not have that power. 9At one time I lived without
understanding the law. But when I learned the command not to covet, for instance,
the power of sin came to life, 10and I died. So I discovered that the law's commands,
which were supposed to bring life, brought spiritual death instead. 11Sin took
advantage of those commands and deceived me; it used the commands to kill me.*

How do these words of Paul affirm the idea that knowledge does not mean control?

When I think back on my twenty-five-year marriage, I knew we had problems, but it seemed like any attempt I made to solve them never worked. We were too afraid of what others would think and, honestly, too broke to get outside help. So being the dutiful Christian couple, we just doubled down, polished our masks, and poured into our kids. I can only speak for myself, but on most days I felt like a failure as a wife, so instead I determined to be the best mother a girl could be. If I couldn't control my marriage, I would control my kids. I wasn't happy, but dang it, I was going to make sure that my children were. My kids were pretty amazing on their own, but if the world wasn't turning in their favor on a given day, I had the charisma and determination to change its trajectory. If I'm being honest, my ex-husband and I did our best to solve all of their problems and influence most of their decisions, but by doing that, we unknowingly set ourselves up as gods in their lives.

Well, my marriage didn't make it, and the images we built crumbled. I'm not kidding when I say we entered a season of tumors and plagues. My adult children felt their lives melting away, and they ended up with what they considered to be a mere shadow of the life they were "supposed" to have—and lucky me got a front row seat. I will tell you that in the last three years, I have grown in knowledge like you can't imagine. Knowledge about myself (more than I ever really wanted!). Knowledge about my children. Knowledge about psychology, personalities, chronic illness, and the grace of God. Yet, with all this newfound knowledge, I have gained very little control. Matter of fact, the more knowledge I have gained, the more control I have relinquished to God.

Hear me when I say that a time will come when you can't make your children's decisions (or anyone else's) or solve their problems. All you may have is knowledge (sometimes too much), understanding, and compassion—yet very little control. When that time comes, you will see pain and desperation in their eyes, partly because they too will realize that you cannot fix this one with a kiss and a band-aid, a parent teacher conference, or a check. You will feel so helpless—and you may wish you had allowed them more time to work out their own faith and build their own faith muscles. You may wish that there had been more times when you had just gotten out of the way.

Yet, God desperately loves us. Yet, God! Don't you love those words? None of this came as a surprise to Him. He has both knowledge and control—all of which is wrapped in the most beautiful package of grace. He has a plan for you. Release your grip. Leave your broken graven image on the floor and watch Him work!

It is amazing to me that the Philistines, of all people, recognized quickly that things were out of their control, and they chose to release their grip on their "trophy."

Read 1 Samuel 6:7-12. What plan did the Philistines come up with to send the ark back to the land of the Israelites?

Extra Insight

When mama cows are separated from their babies, they make a higher pitched, louder call meant to alert their calves that they are being missed.[16]

Setting things right requires us to focus on God over the ones we love.

Do you think the natural instinct of a milk cow would be to walk away from her young? Of course not! This was the point. The Philistines needed to know if the God of Israel was truly behind all of the painful events they had been experiencing or if it was just bad luck. To know for sure, they set up a scenario that would go against nature. A mama cow would never walk away from her young, who had been caged away from her, knowing the calf needed her milk to survive. Yet that is exactly what happened. It didn't just happen with one cow, but two.

The two mama cows, who had never been yoked, walked in unison straight to the land of Israel. Scripture says they lowed as they went. As a mom, this part breaks me! Two different things were pulling at their hearts, and although the one was greater, the lesser still hurt. Their lowing was the sound of sacrifice.

In order to set things right, there had to be sacrifice. It is interesting to note that the sacrifices thus far in 1 Samuel have come from mothers—first Hannah and now the milk cows. Setting things right requires us to focus on God over the ones we love. Sometimes when we choose to do what is right over what is easy, there is lots of lowing.

Prayer Prompt

Ask God to show you areas in your life you try to control. Prayerfully consider if all of your striving has been beneficial or simply taking the ark from city to city—in other words, putting out one fire just to start another. When we feel out of control in one area, we tend to seek control in others. Journal about what trusting God would look like in your specific situation.

DAY 5

Yesterday we ended our lesson with the sound of lowing ringing in our ears, and today we resume the story with those same cows making their way into an Israelite village. Imagine the people working in the fields when, all of a sudden, they hear what sounds like cattle lowing. When they lift their eyes, they see two milk cows—no doubt engorged with milk—yoked together and pulling the ark of God on a cart. I would have loved to see their faces—the faces of the people, not the cows, that is!

Read 1 Samuel 6:13-21. What was the name of the village? Where did the cart stop?

Before we move on—and trust me, you won't mind waiting—let's learn a little bit about this place. Beth-shemesh was a levitical city set aside for the clan of Kohath as recorded in Joshua 21:13-16. Stick with me here. I promise it will make a difference in our understanding of this story.

Read Numbers 4:1-15. What specific job was given to the house of Kohath?

So, let's tie this together. The two cows, despite their natural instinct to stay with their calves, brought the ark of the covenant straight to a levitical city. Not only did priests live in this area but also the very family who had been given the responsibility to care for the holy things inside the Tabernacle—the ark being the greatest of them all. So, if anyone knew how to treat the ark of the covenant with reverence, it would have been these very people or the group of priests among them.

What did they do first after discovering the ark (1 Samuel 6:14-15)?

Scripture Focus

1 Samuel 6:13-21

Extra Insight

The Levites were descendants of Jacob's son, Levi. God set this clan apart to serve God. When the Tabernacle was created (Exodus 25–31, 35–40), the Levites were responsible for disassembling, transporting, and reconstructing the tabernacle when the Israelites traveled.[17]

I know, right? This is so heartbreaking. Not only did these mama cows sacrifice by leaving their calves behind and carrying the ark of God back to His people, but they literally became the sacrifice once the people received it. There is nothing fair about this situation and, honestly, nothing holy.

Read Leviticus 1:3. According to this verse, what were the requirements of a burnt offering?

You got it! A *male* from the herd without spot or blemish. What about a milk cow made them think *male* or without blemish? I'm sorry, but I didn't make it through childbirth without a few blemishes! What about you? The very ones who should have known how to handle the ark and make sacrifices did not do it properly! Just another example of the compromise within the priesthood. Well, the lords of the Philistines saw all they needed to see, so they went back home; and frankly, I am glad they did. For what comes next would have sent them home with more questions than answers. When the people of God misuse the things of God, the consequences can really bring confusion to outsiders.

I am sure the Israelites came from all over to see this miraculous return of the ark back to them. There must have been great fanfare when they pulled the graven images from the cart one by one, describing what they were and which city they were from. I can just hear the shouting as each city of the Philistines was called out by name, none of which was spared from God's judgment. Yet, then we read something that makes us recoil. Their celebration soon turned to weeping.

Reread 1 Samuel 6:19-20, also reading Numbers 3:4 for context clues. What happened in these verses?

Why did they suffer this fate?

When the ark was not within the Tabernacle, it was to be covered by at least three coverings—the veil leading into the Holy of Holies, a cover of animal skins, and a cloth of solid blue (Numbers 4:4-7). Commentators question whether the Israelites merely uncovered the ark for all to see or if some-one actually attempted to look inside. (Even Indiana Jones knew better than that!) We don't know. Either action was prohibited and punishable by death.

Depending on the Bible translation you consult, you will learn that any-where from seventy to fifty thousand people died that day. However, most scholars think about seventy people perished because Beth-shemesh was a small town.[18,19] But what is even more interesting to me is the Israelites' response to this deadly event:

> "Who is able to stand before the LORD, this holy God? And to whom shall he go up away from us?"
>
> (1 Samuel 6:20)

Well, the answer to the first question is *nobody*! We see this several places in Scripture:

> "But," he [God] said, "you cannot see my face, for man shall not see me and live."
> (Exodus 33:20)

> No one has ever seen God, but the one and only Son, who is Himself God and is at the Father's side, has made Him known.
>
> (John 1:18 BSB)

> [He] who alone has immortality, who dwells in unapproachable light, whom no one has ever seen or can see. To him be honor and eternal dominion. Amen.
> (1 Timothy 6:16)

No one can see God and live! Therefore, God sent His Son Jesus, being fully God yet fully flesh. Jesus, the Living Word, reveals God to us. Think about it. When you speak, your words reveal who you are. If you want to get to know someone, you talk and have relationship. If you want to know God, look to Jesus. Jesus is the full expression of God in flesh and blood. Colossians 2:9 says that in Him the fullness of deity (God) dwells.

Let's take another look at John 1:18. The NIV puts it this way: "No one has ever seen God, but the one and only Son, who is himself God and is in closest relationship with the Father, has made him known." Jesus, being in the closest relationship with His Father, has made God known to us.

How does this relate to our study today? Just as Jesus points to God, so the ark points to Jesus. Explore this with me. It was made out of acacia wood (Exodus 25:10). This makes practical sense considering acacia trees would have been the most readily available material in the area. Yet there are those who also believe that acacia wood is resistant to decay, offering another reason for the selection.[20] In the desert terrain, the acacia also

If you want to know God, look to Jesus. Jesus is the full expression of God in flesh and blood.

produces thorns for protection against drought.[21] It doesn't take much to see the beautiful picture of Jesus and His humanity in this symbolism. The body of Jesus saw no decay because he remained in the tomb for only three days, and he bore the curse of thorns on His brow.

The acacia wood was covered in gold, representing Jesus's deity (Exodus 25:11).[22] The covering, the Mercy Seat, was made out of one solid piece of gold that was beaten to form a covering with two cherubim on either end, whose wings stretched out over the seat (Exodus 25:17-20). They seemed to offer some kind of shade or protection over the mercy seat. Never lifting their eyes away from the place where, once a year, blood would be sprinkled for the atonement of the nation. I am sure you have already picked up on the symbolism of the "beating" connected to the death of Jesus, but I also want you to see something really cool.

Read John 20:11-12. How many angels were in the tomb of Jesus when Mary looked in? Where were they seated?

Here we have the mercy seat depicted in the tomb. The body of Jesus had lain between the two angels—His blood sprinkled on the greatest mercy seat for all. He had fulfilled the law, and through a new covenant of His blood, He would usher in grace. Those are but a few of the amazing things about the ark that point to Jesus.

Of course, we can see these representations because we have the full revelation of Scripture, but these Old Testament characters would not have understood them. Yet in His great love, God stooped to give them earthly representations of a future mystery—the mystery of grace through the blood of Jesus.

Considering what it represented, the ark was to be treated with the utmost respect. But instead, the people of Israel treated it with contempt. The sad fact is that despite their proximity to the law, they didn't understand the consequences any more than the Philistines.

When people encountered Jesus, they often came to the same conclusion as the Philistines did. If we can't control it, we don't want it. Send it away!

Let's look to a New Testament story and consider similarities. Read Mark 5:1-20. What do the people do in verse 17?

The Gentiles living on the north side of the Sea of Galilee, in the area called the Decapolis, had been dealing with a demon-possessed man for years. They could not control him. They could not bind him. All they could do was stay away from him as he inhabited the tombs, screaming out twenty-four-seven. I am sure they could not even bear to look at him with the deep bloody wounds covering his naked, dirty body. Jesus came to their land and met this man straight away. He had just calmed the storm, showing His disciples that He was the God of creation. He was the God of everything "natural." Now He would show them and any onlookers that He was also the God of everything "supernatural." Jesus calmed the possessed man. He cast out the demons, the man breathed in peace, and like the sea, he was still!

Yet, verse 17 tells us that when the people of the town came and saw what had happened, they wanted Jesus to leave. What? Yes. They must have wondered, *Who could be stronger than the demons? If we could not control this wild man, we definitely cannot control* Him. This power that they did not know and could not control scared them more than the demons! *Please go away from us, Jesus.* When a person encounters a holy God, his or her instinct is to hide. Just ask Adam and Eve (Genesis 3).

This story about the Israelites looking upon the ark reminds me of a belief I learned as a child, that God is too pure to look upon sin (Habakkuk 1:13). I can still hear the pastor yelling, "God hates sin!" The problem was that in my mind, *sin* and *sinner* were synonymous, which left me feeling shame. I believed the only reason God could bare to look at me was that He was actually seeing His son instead of me. Like some holy decoupage, I was hidden by Jesus. Later I began to realize the implication of Jesus's divinity. As the full expression of God, He not only looked upon sinners, He also ate with them, touched them, and seemed to delight in them. He wasn't repulsed by them; He was drawn to them—not to camouflage them or cover them, but to cleanse them and set them free from hiding.

The truth is, we aren't hidden *from* God, we're hidden *in* God. We aren't hidden *by* Christ; we're hidden *with* Christ (Colossians 3:3). In Jesus, we have been reconciled. He sees us. He delights in us. He wants a relationship with us. In his book *Ragamuffin Gospel*, Brennan Manning explores how God's love is always an open-armed invitation back into authentic relationship, one in which His love sees us as we are and not as we should be.[23] God never sends us away. I don't believe that sin keeps God from us, but it keeps us from God. And that's good news.

Prayer Prompt

What is keeping you from a deep connection with your Father right now? Consider not only your behaviors but also your beliefs. Are you assuming things about God that may not be true? Are you giving Him motives that He doesn't have? Are you assuming all the voices or judgments in your head are from God? Could they be from you instead? Be reconciled with God. Don't send Him away. Talk to Him.

Video Viewer Guide: Week 1

God is always at _____. He is always in _____.

Our worth is not found in what we _____, produce, or achieve. It is found in the heart of _____.

Comparison highlights our _____.

The only One who can fill your _____ _____ is the One who knit you together in your mother's womb.

_____ are the indicators of what is going on inside of us, but we are not _____ to them.

Life is hard, but God has fully _____ us with everything we need to get through it.

Anything that is out of our control is still within _____.

Scriptures: 1 Samuel 1:1-7, Psalm 143:8, 1 Samuel 2:1-10, Romans 15:4, Genesis 2:1, 1 Samuel 1:19-20

Week 2

I've Got This Under Control

Maintaining the Façade

1 Samuel 7–12

DAY 1

We concluded Week 1 with the end of 1 Samuel 6. Somewhere in between the events of chapters 6 and 7, the Israelites apparently have come under the domination of the Philistines. Let's begin today by diving into the Scripture.

Scripture Focus

1 Samuel 7:1-11; 8:1-9

Read 1 Samuel 7:1-6, and answer the following questions:

How did the people show that they had turned back to the Lord?

Who interceded for them? (v. 5)

Verse 2 reminds us that the ark has remained in Kiriath-jearim for twenty years, suggesting God's hand of protection still remained lifted from His people. That's a long time! The ark, the symbol of His presence, remained hidden away in some dark room instead of in its place of prominence in the Tabernacle radiating the glory of God.

At the end of those twenty years, the Israelites mourned and cried for God. They prayed for His return and probably wondered, *Would God remain silent forever? Was He still angry?* The last time they had seen the ark, so many had lost their lives.

Samuel, now grown, was their go-to guy. He was their priest, prophet, and emerging judge, so he answered the petitions of the people (v. 3). To be honest, when I read the instructions Samuel gave the people, I have an attitude of resistance. There just seem to be so many "if-then" statements in the Old Testament, as if God is saying, "If you do this for Me, then I will do this for you." It's the old "obedience leads to blessing" idea. But we have to remember that the Israelites have entered into a covenant relationship with God, much like our marriage covenant. After treating God like an ordinary object at Beth-shemesh, they sent the ark (and God's presence) away. Instead of evaluating their part in the catastrophe, they cast God off. Instead of repenting for making a mockery of their relationship, they basically told Him to leave.

Now the people give lip service about wanting God back, yet they had made no changes to indicate they had repentant hearts. They said they wanted Him back, but they had been cheating on Him for twenty years and had made no attempt to stop seeing their mistresses, their idols. Samuel's plea, then, is not about God rejecting them for any legalistic behaviors. This is not conditional love. This is about them abusing their relationship partner. And we all know that relationships are always two-way streets.

God was essentially saying, "Do you want a real relationship with me or not? If both of us are not committed to this relationship, then it is not going to work properly. Remember our vows! We committed to an exclusive relationship. My love is longsuffering, and I am willing to wait for you for as long as it takes. Yet, let me be clear, I will not share you with another. I am a jealous God" (Exodus 34:14). God's jealousy is not a vice but a healthy zeal for His people. Isn't it amazing how hard relationships are? Even here the relationship is hard, and one of the parties is God!

Under the mediation of Samuel, the people assembled at Mizpah. They poured out water on the ground before the Lord, symbolizing their repentance. I can just hear the sound of the water pouring out like tears before God as they confessed their sins and regrets. This scene reminds me of the desert of Phoenix, Arizona, where I live. The monsoons come and pour down rain on the dry, scorched ground. The air is so fresh the next day and the sky so clear. Where there is sincere repentance, there is opportunity for new growth, new breath, and new beginnings!

On the heels of this revival, the Israelites must face a familiar enemy. It is amazing to me how, after an experience such as this, there is always resistance! Very often when we choose to do the right thing or make things right, the situation can seem to get worse before it gets better. It's as if the pressure increases just to see how committed we are to stay the course. In our narrative, this pushback came from the Philistines. They heard the nation of Israel had assembled in one place, and they saw this as an amazing opportunity to wipe the Israelites from the planet.

> God's jealousy is not a vice but a healthy zeal for His people.

Read 1 Samuel 7:7-9. What happened when Israel got word about the impending Philistine attack? What was their initial response, and then what did they do?

The Israelites were afraid. Of course they were! When you have been poured out like a drink offering, you feel a little vulnerable. You are not quite prepared to take a punch. The people cried out to Samuel and trusted him to intervene on their behalf. Samuel faithfully performed his role as their priest (mediator), petitioning on behalf of his people and asking God to rescue them.

Do you have one or more people in your life who are in a vulnerable time right now? Those who have humbled themselves, hoping that the love of God is longsuffering and the people of God are forgiving. Those who need your encouragement, love, and prayers. Have you been faithful to be God's agent of grace and show them the reckless love of God? Write briefly about how you have been or can be an agent of grace in their lives.

If we were watching this story in 1 Samuel 7 on the big screen, we would be biting our fingernails by verse 10. Talk about coming down to the wire! While Samuel was still performing the sacrifices, the Philistines attacked. But don't sweat it, because we are about to see the promise of Matthew 6:8 in action—our God knows what we need even before we ask it.

Read 1 Samuel 7:10-11. How did God answer Samuel's request?

God answered Samuel's request just in time with a voice of thunder that caused confusion.

In Hebrew, the name
Beth-car means
"place of a lamb."[1]

———————

The word "remember"
is mentioned over 130
times in the Bible (KJV).[2]

The King has returned! (Cue the music.) It's like watching a movie where the enemy army is about to strike the first deadly blow, but something super-natural stops them and causes them to turn on each other. Can you see the shock on the Israelites' faces? Can you hear the battle cry as they turn and chase the Philistines, defeating them as far as Beth-car?

Listen, God is never late, but sometimes He cuts it really close! Knowing the people's tendency to forget, Samuel set up a reminder for them, placing a remembrance stone between Mizpah and Shen (1 Samuel 7:12). I can totally relate because the older I get, the more I forget appointments, names, words, and anything else you can imagine. Can you relate?

This stone also marked the edge of Israel's newly acquired territory. Samuel named it Ebenezer, meaning, "Thus far has the Lord helped us." Thus far? Does this insinuate that they have more territory to conquer? You bet your Ebenezer! When it comes to blessing, God is no Scrooge! Actually, under the leadership of Samuel, they would take back the Philistine cities from Ekron to Gath; they provided support to neighboring nations as well as freed them from Philistine oppression (v. 14), a reminder that God always blesses us so we can be a blessing to others.

After twenty long years of oppression, Israel finally had peace. Samuel shepherded his nation by making yearly rounds, keeping God in the forefront of their lives (v. 16). When he wasn't making rounds, his door was always open in Ramah, his home town; it was from here that he judged Israel and built an altar to the Lord (v. 17).

Read 1 Samuel 8:1-9. Why did the elders of Israel decide to meet with Samuel? What did they want and why? (vv. 4-5)

I'm going to be honest with you. If I had been on that elder board, I would have done the same thing. History had proven (for four hundred years) that when Israel failed to have a strong leader, destruction was coming.

Samuel was old. The elders not only recognized this, but also saw that Samuel's sons were not walking in his ways. Yet, Samuel appointed his sons as judges! I wonder: did God actually want him to do so? We don't know if Samuel's sons started being dishonest after they were appointed or had questionable character before then. If it was the latter, then Samuel should have known better. For goodness sake, he grew up with Hophni and Phinehas! Perhaps the people wondered if dishonesty was a trend for leaders' kids.

The elders saw a storm coming, so they asked for a king. Why a king and not a judge? Possibly, they had seen in the other nations around them the value of having one united nation led by one king. They might have believed this to be the best thing for the security and survival of their nation.

Before we judge the elders too harshly, let's read Genesis 17:6; 35:11; and 49:10. What hint or foreshadowing do these verses contain?

The Scriptures suggest that one day Israel would have a king. Yet, I Samuel 8:7 clearly states that their request for a king was a rejection of God. How do we bring these Scriptures into agreement?

Could this actually be more about the lack of trust beneath the request than the object of it? If God had predicted a king, wasn't it His job to determine the appropriate time and person? Did He need the elders' plans and petitions? No, God was not caught unaware of the vulnerable situation Israel was in.

Maybe the people wanted a king they could control and maneuver, much like the maneuvering of the ark in the previous chapters. Perhaps even a king the other nations could see and fear. They might have wanted to build an earthly kingdom much like Babel, a kingdom that would boast their own power and dominion instead of God's. Once again, in order to understand what's going on, let's focus on who's trying to run the show.

If the Israelites had trusted God, would He not have provided them with a king in His time, one of His choosing and filled with His Spirit? After all, He had never let them down when they had waited on and trusted in Him. We know from Genesis 49:10 (see the margin) that God's king would come from the tribe of Judah. Ultimately, King David, the man after God's own heart (1 Samuel 13:14; Acts 13:22), would be chosen by God to reign. As promised, his kingdom will be eternal through Jesus.

This was more about the battle for control than a simple request for a king. They would soon realize what this request would cost them. They would not gain power but lose it instead.

Chapter 7 began with the people pouring out their repentance to God, and by chapter 8 they were demanding a king. They had lost their total dependency on God. How did that happen? May I suggest time and comfort. With the exodus in the distant past, they had become too comfortable in the Promised Land. Instead of life being about a relationship with God, (Philippians 1:21), they thought living was about gain and they only turned to God when their

The scepter shall not depart from Judah,
nor the ruler's staff from between his feet,
until tribute comes to him;
and to him shall be the obedience of the peoples.
(Genesis 49:10)

While comfort may seem like the road to take, it is often the enemy.

lives were threatened. When all seemed lost, they trusted God. But when all seemed possible, they trusted themselves. May we learn from their example. While comfort may seem like the road to take, it is often the enemy.

Prayer Prompt

Meditate on Matthew 16:25, and ask God to reveal the ways you are attempting to "save" your life. What would it look like to "lose" it? What are you afraid of losing by choosing God over control and comfort? Did you enter into a relationship with Jesus only to secure eternal life, or were you looking for a life-long partner? Talk with Him, asking for discernment about when to engage and when to release control.

DAY 2

Scripture Focus

1 Samuel 8:10-22;
9:1-27; 10:1

Yesterday we saw that the Israelites lost their dependence on God and begged Samuel for a king. Today's lesson begins with a reality check from their beloved prophet.

Read 1 Samuel 8:10-18, and list below the things Samuel warned them about having a king.

In their attempt to *gain* control, the Israelites would soon realize they had actually *relinquished* it. When a person becomes king or queen, he or she builds an earthly kingdom. Guess how? Yep! With your money. Taxes! Building a kingdom is expensive, and defending one is too. Samuel warned them that a king would take not only their money but also their sons for his army and their daughters for workers in his palace.

Listen, government costs money to build and maintain. Along with that, it often requires blood to defend it. The power of government will always come at the cost of individual freedom. Yet, often in its absence there is anarchy. The trick is finding the perfect balance between the two in order to provide for national security and the people's well-being.

The Israelites would learn in the future that when people are in power, very often there is corruption. We see this throughout their history. What the

Israelites had forgotten is that they had the perfect King, and in Him there is no corruption. With Him there is no need to build a kingdom; it is *all* His. He requires no defense, and His desire for His people is freedom.

The next verses in 1 Samuel 8 are some of the most foreboding verses in the Bible.

Read 1 Samuel 8:19-22. What does God tell Samuel in verse 22?

In a nutshell, God tells Samuel to "give them what they want." Oh friend, we need to be careful what we ask for. God may just give it to us. It may be the only way for us to finally realize what we actually need.

Now read 1 Samuel 9:1-2, and list the attributes of Saul.

It seems as if God Himself hand picks Saul to be the king. Yet later, Samuel's words in 1 Samuel 12:13 profess that Saul was actually the people's choice. Both are true! Saul was the cream of the crop in Israel. If the elders had gone throughout the land looking for a king, they would have found no one better than Saul, according to earthly standards. They would have chosen him themselves. God knew what they wanted, and He gave it to them. No fanfare required.

Saul was the tall, dark, and handsome son of a powerful man from the tribe of Benjamin. Sounds like Prince Charming to me. According to every outside measurement, Saul had it all. He was the stud walking down the hall in his letterman's jacket who scored the winning touchdown at Friday night's game. Saul looked like a king. When facing their enemies, Saul would be sure to stand out, for he stood head and shoulders above every other Israelite.

What does 1 Samuel 16:7 (in the margin) say about outer appearance?

We all have the propensity to judge others based on outer appearance. I cannot be the only woman who makes quick judgments based on clothes, hair, purses, jewelry, homes, physique, and so forth. We may not speak them, stick to them, or discriminate because of them, but we make them.

Extra Insight

Great height was valued in a king in ancient times and in eastern countries.[3]

But the LORD said to Samuel, "Do not look on his appearance or on the height of his stature, because I have rejected him. For the LORD sees not as man sees: man looks on the outward appearance, but the LORD looks on the heart."

(1 Samuel 16:7)

Our assumptions may not be bad, good, or even correct, but they are made! Often, we find out that many of our assumptions are wrong. Appearances can betray.

The Hebrew word for "clothes" is *begadim*. Its singular term is *beged*, and it comes from the root word *boged*, which means "traitor, one who has broken faith."[4] What does *betrayal* have to do with clothes? It wasn't until Adam and Eve "broke faith" with God and realized they were naked that we have the first reference to clothes/coverings in Scripture, found in Genesis 3:7. The Hebrew word here is different because the emphasis is on the inadequacy of the covering. Yet the idea still applies. When Adam and Eve became aware of their state, they immediately covered their vulnerabilities.

It is also interesting to consider how clothing was used in the stories of both Jacob and Joseph. Jacob betrayed his father into thinking he was Esau by covering his skin with goat skins (Genesis 27). Joseph's brothers betrayed their father by convincing him that Joseph was dead using his multicolored robe (Genesis 37).

In other places in Scripture, clothes symbolize purity and dignity, such as the high priestly garments. In their case, the clothes really did make the man. So, clothes can communicate about us, but they can also deceive. We may be able to deceive others with outer appearance, but we cannot deceive ourselves.

Look into the mirror right now. Have an honest conversation with yourself. Who are you *really*? What do you want, and where do you want to go?

In what ways does your outer appearance speak truth about you, and in what ways is it an attempt to cover up your insecurities?

We may be able to deceive others with outer appearance, but we cannot deceive ourselves.

Outer appearance may fool others, but it won't fool the most important person: *you*! Deep in our hearts we know the insecurities we seek to cover. Don't let them hold you hostage any longer. Be who you are, and let it show!

Okay, back to Saul.

Read 1 Samuel 9:3-10, and write below any assumptions we might make about Saul.

When I read verse 3, I can't help but laugh. My first thought is, I *have an idea who might have lost those donkeys*! My son would have totally fit the bill of prospective king. He was the handsome jock wearing the letterman's jacket walking down the halls of his high school. He was the one who scored the winning touchdown at Friday night's game. He was the one who made the girls all weak in the knees, but he also was the one who would have left the stinking gate open, allowing the donkeys to escape.

I wonder if this is the reason Saul's dad, Kish, made him go look for the donkeys—because perhaps he was the one responsible for losing them. Donkeys were the "work truck" of the farm. They were an important piece of equipment, and they also were considered valuable.[5] They were so important that dignitaries often rode on them.[6] Kish was not going to allow them to disappear without a search. The donkeys were out there somewhere, and they would have his mark of ownership on them. Whether or not Saul was responsible for losing the donkeys, he was commissioned to find them.

To me, the narrator seems to be painting a picture of a son who was learning to take over the family business. Imagine that scenario with me. Kish sent out his pride and joy to find his donkeys. This was not a hard job, often done by a servant or slave, but it was time for Saul to assume his position in the family. It was time for Saul to learn what it takes to run a business. It was time for Saul to prove himself responsible. Could it have been that Kish was giving Saul some responsibility but not too much—giving him some rope—but not enough to hang himself with?

It was unsafe for people to travel alone in those days, and as a parent, I can understand how Kish might have wanted to send a trustworthy, experienced servant along with his son.

It's interesting that after three days Saul was willing to come home without the donkeys. Is it possible that at this point things might have started to get difficult, considering their rations were running out (v. 7)? Perhaps difficult was not something Saul was used to. Was Saul willing to go the extra mile to get the job done? Had Saul grown up with such privilege that a few donkeys were expendable? Or was Saul merely concerned that his father might worry about them? Either way, when the pressure was applied to Saul, what would it reveal?

The servant, however, was not so quick to return. He told Saul of a prophet who lived in the area and suggested they go ask him for help. The experience of the servant was shining through. Saul followed the servant's lead.

What happened next in verses 11-14? (Is there anything about verse 11 that makes you laugh?)

Like I said earlier, when it came to looks, my son had the lion's share. It was not uncommon for me to walk into a restaurant with him and see every young girl turn her head. So, when I read that Saul ran into a group of young girls going out to draw water, I am not surprised that the girls were willing to stop and chat. They were more than willing to help a brother out.

Read 1 Samuel 9:15-20, and put yourself in Samuel's shoes. He was now old and had been leading Israel his whole life. He was looking upon the young man whom God had chosen to replace him. What might he have been thinking? What would you have been thinking?

When Saul had set out three days before to find the lost donkeys, he had no idea that he would return home as the anointed king of Israel. He had come with one worry on his mind: "Where are my father's donkeys?" This just goes to show that very often we worry about things that just don't matter in the big picture.

According to verse 20, were the donkeys lost?

When have you realized that you worried about things that didn't matter and failed to focus on things that did?

Samuel relieved Saul's worry regarding the donkeys by telling him that they had been found. Yet, his words in verse 20 also suggest a greater challenge was on the horizon. He basically said, "Saul, while your mind has been on donkeys, 'all the desire of Israel' (NIV) has been on you."

Read 1 Samuel 9:21-24.

What was Saul's objection?

How did Samuel respond? What did he do for Saul?

It sounds like Saul had just won the lottery. B*ut had he*? If you thought finding donkeys was a hard job, try shepherding Israel!

Let's conclude today by reading 1 Samuel 9:25-27 and 10:1. What do we witness here?

Extra Insight

Saul means "asked of God." Israel asked for a king, and Saul became their choice.[7]

I wish I could hear all that Samuel shared with Saul on the edge of town that day, but it was a private message. I cannot imagine what was running through the mind of Saul as the oil ran down his head and the voice of Samuel proclaimed: "Has not the Lord anointed you ruler over his inheritance?" (1 Samuel 10:1 NIV).

The nation wanted control. They wanted a king. And God gave them a young man who literally couldn't seem to find his own "ass"! (Now, that's funny!) Listen, I am not judging poor Saul because I can totally relate. I often wonder why God called me to teach His Word. You are probably thinking the same thing considering my last statement, but what I do know is that God can be trusted! Sometimes it doesn't seem so, based on our circumstances, but just remember, life can change in a moment. When you have no idea how things are ever going to work out, remember Saul out looking for donkeys and coming home with a crown.

Prayer Prompt

Spend some time pouring out your worries to God. He knows them anyway! Write them down, because there is something about getting them out of your brain and onto paper. Now, visualize handing each one over to

When you have no idea how things are ever going to work out, remember Saul out looking for donkeys and coming home with a crown.

God. Sometimes we think trusting God is simply releasing our burdens, but if you're holding a heavy weight over your head, releasing it would not be smart. We need to *hand it off*. Hand over your burdens to God and trust that He has a plan for your good and His glory!

DAY 3

Scripture Focus

1 Samuel 10:2-24

I cannot imagine what was going through Saul's mind as he left Samuel to reunite with his servant. How could all of this be true? Israel had never had a king. Why now? Why him? What must he do to be king? What on earth would he tell his father? I am sure his questions were endless. Knowing me, I would have been in the "what if" mindset for days!

When doubt fills our minds, we search desperately for any sign of confirmation. In Saul's case, he didn't have to search at all. Samuel told him in advance that he would see three signs confirming what had just happened.

Read 1 Samuel 10:2-7. Below you will find locations from the text. Match them with the signs that would occur at each place.

_____ 1. Rachel's tomb at Zelzah

_____ 2. Oak of Tabor

_____ 3. Gilbeath-elohim

A. Saul would meet a group of prophets, the Spirit of the Lord would rush upon Saul, and he would prophesy.

B. Saul would meet two men who would tell him that the donkeys had been found and his father Kish was anxious about him.

C. Saul would meet two men who would give him three loaves of bread.

These signs confirmed that God can find what's lost, provide for our needs, and change us from the inside out. When all the people saw what happened to Saul, they asked, "What is this that has happened to the son of Kish? Is Saul also among the prophets?" (1 Samuel 10:11 NIV). They could not believe what they saw. Had Saul found God? Was he a changed man?

How can we read this story without seeing the beauty of the gospel? I am not saying this is a purposeful type or shadow, but here I see the parallel as I read this story. Like Saul, we go about our lives searching for what we think is lost, when all along it is we who are lost. Through God's divine providence, He directs our steps to some "prophet" who speaks life changing words to us. It could be a coach, a teacher, or a neighbor. And, as in 1 Samuel 9:19 (NIV), they tell us "all that is in [our] heart." When we hear the words of salvation, we realize that this is what we have been longing for all along and didn't know it. We are no longer lost, but now we are found. God sees us and He loves us. He has provided a way for our salvation through the body and blood of Jesus on the cross—the bread and the wine, just as Saul was given bread and wine (1 Samuel 10:3-4). When we accept this gift, we are filled with the Spirit of God and we become new people. And as others see this change, they wonder, "What has happened to Shannon? Is she also among the prophets?"

> Take a moment to look back at your journey to salvation. Remember the circumstances and the people God used to influence you along the way. Make some notes below. You might even want to take time to write a note to thank one of these special people.

> Now read 1 Samuel 10:14-16. Why do you think Saul chose not to tell his family about his anointing?

Saul may have had a new heart, but his journey was just beginning. How do you explain something that you truly don't understand yourself? Can you imagine the questions his family would have had? Likely, Saul was not prepared to give any answers.

> Read 1 Samuel 10:17-21 and summarize what happened.

It was time to go public. Samuel called all the people of Israel together at Mizpah. There must have been quite the buzz in the air. Was Samuel going to give them what they wanted? Was Samuel going to announce the name of their king?

The old prophet began his speech by giving credit where credit was due. He wanted the people to understand that their request for a king was a rejection of their God. God had freed them from bondage, bound Himself to them in a covenant relationship, and faithfully protected them from their enemies. He did all of this even when Israel consistently proved unfaithful.

Why is it that so often we project our issues onto others? The Israelites had no reason to doubt or mistrust God. He had never been unfaithful to them. The problem was within them. Yet, they continued to look outwardly to solve an inward problem.

> Read 1 Samuel 10:20-21 and Joshua 7:14-18. What do these verses have in common? What is different?

The nation of Israel was organized and identified by tribes and families within those tribes. Samuel had the tribes come together, and he cast lots to reveal their first king. Casting lots involved the use of small objects, such as sticks, flat stones, or some kind of dice (see Extra Insight).[8] They were somehow used to determine yes and no answers or often guilt or innocence. The closest similarity is flipping a coin. Samuel used this method to dwindle down his choice from tribe to family to individual. Saul had already been anointed by Samuel, yet this was an opportunity for God to reveal the king to the people. Samuel was merely the mouthpiece of God in this instance and would not be held personally accountable for this choice.

To be honest, there are times I wish I could get my hands on that Urim and Thummim (see Extra Insight). How about you? I remember a time in my own life when I simply asked God for a yes or no answer. My children grew up going to Christian school through the eighth grade. I was the Bible teacher on campus, and for the most part it was an ideal situation. (More for me possibly than for them, because it's hard being a teacher's kid sometimes.) Yet, there came a time when their father and I had to decide if our son, who was the oldest, would remain there for high school or go to a public school. Zach was an exceptional athlete, and we knew that in order for him to excel in sports he probably needed a larger arena. We agonized over this decision for months. We spent time listing the pros and cons, constantly feeling the pressure from

Extra Insight

The Old Testament mentions specific lots called Urim and Thummim in Exodus 28:30 in reference to the high priest's garments. "On the high priest's ephod (an apron-like garment) lay a breastpiece…a pouch inlaid with 12 precious stones engraved with the names of the 12 tribes of Israel… that held the Urim and Thummim."[9]

our family and school community. When making the decision, it literally felt like Zach's future relied on it. (This makes me laugh now!) We wanted Zach's dreams to come true. At least that is what we told ourselves. I question now if this was more about his dreams or ours.

I finally suggested that we shelf the whole idea for a while and simply pray that God would just give us a yes or no answer. You know, throw out the Urim and Thummim. I said, "God knows what Zach needs. He knows the future and we do not. Can't we just trust His yes or no?" We stopped talking about it for two weeks but continued to pray, and we scheduled a date night two weeks out to come together and share what God had revealed to us individually. (I'm not saying this is what everyone should do, but this is just what we did.) After two weeks, we went out for dinner and gave our answers. We both felt God leading Zach to public school. This decision caused all kinds of stress in our family life and my professional life, but we were confident in our choice. God had said yes.

My son went on to become one of the most highly-sought-after athletes in the state of Arizona his senior year. He became a two-sport star for Stanford University, playing both football and baseball. He was drafted by the Arizona Diamondbacks in 2016. His athletic accomplishments were amazing, but they came at a high cost to his body and soul.

Looking back now, I realize that we may have turned to God in pivotal moments, appearing very spiritual, but when it came down to it, we were still sailing the ship. We had charted our own course. We asked God for immediate yes or no directions, but we didn't want His opinion about our overall plan. The engines were full throttle. The last thing we were willing to do was to slow down and listen. If we did that, we would lose all momentum, and we really didn't want to hear anything other than "all systems are go." We wanted what we wanted! We wanted Zach to go pro, and he had all the talent to get there.

Sports was king at our house. We prioritized it with our time, our talents, and our treasures. In many ways, sports kept us united. It entertained us. It promoted us. To be honest, it distracted us. We were so focused on reaching "our" destination that we ignored the warnings, "Iceberg ahead!" By every outside standard, we were the Titanic family—unsinkable. But, we sank! When it comes to icebergs, you only see what is above the water, but the part that sinks the ship lies beneath. Even once we sensed what was lurking beneath, we continued to enjoy the music, fine dining, and dancing above. We thought we could outmaneuver it. We were wrong.

Over the last three years, the wreckage has been washing up on shore. I have spent countless hours examining the broken pieces of my life. My broken marriage. My kids' broken hearts and broken dreams. Pieces of

We may have turned to God in pivotal moments, appearing very spiritual, but when it came down to it, we were still sailing the ship.

confusion, fear, entitlement, narcissism, disbelief, shame, brokenness, regret, and betrayal continue to wash up on shore. As I examine each piece, I acknowledge, understand, and forgive. I don't just forgive others but I also forgive myself.

No one purposefully sets out to be shipwrecked. We thought we were doing the right things—at the time. Now, I understand more fully Søren Kierkegaard's famous quotation, "...Life must be understood backwards. But then one forgets the other clause—that it must be lived forwards."[10]

The real problem in Israel was not that they didn't have a king to lead and protect them. The real problem was that they weren't following the one they had—God. They wanted to plot their own course and secure their own future. Their own desired outcome! They wanted to be like the other nations. They sought after the false power and security the world has to offer. They wanted to make a name for themselves. Had they forgotten the story of Babel? Have we?

> Read 1 Samuel 10:21-24. Where was Saul when his name was announced? Put yourself in his shoes and suggest why he might have been there.

When I think of Saul, I can't help but think of icons like Elvis Presley or Marilyn Monroe—everyday people who seemed to be swept away by fame in a moment. Unknown by the world one minute and a household name the next. Not many people can handle such power, fame, and fortune.

Literally, this young man was out looking for lost donkeys one day and the next he was being crowned the king of Israel! Who is ready for that? No wonder he was hiding in the baggage!

> How is God calling you to step up to the plate right now? What baggage of life are you hiding behind? Are you feeling ill-equipped? Unprepared? Write about it briefly below.

God invites us to join Him. Remember He is the "owner," and we are merely the "general managers." God sets the course, and we follow His plan. He makes sure we have the necessary equipment, and we steward it with integrity. His desire then and now is still, "Follow me!" (Matthew 4:19).

Prayer Prompt

Yesterday, we spent time talking to God about our worries. Today I would like you to talk to Him about your direction. Have you already set the course for your life—and perhaps for those you love as well? Is there room in your plan for a godly detour that may lead you to undreamed shores, or are you bent on sailing your originally charted course even if all that survives the voyage is wreckage?

DAY 4

As 1 Samuel 10 comes to a close, we see Saul finally take the stage. With a little help from Samuel, he steps out from behind his—oh, I mean, *the*—baggage and accepts his role as king. Every eye in the nation is on him as they all shout, "Long live the king!" (1 Samuel 10:24). I cannot imagine how nervous and scared he must have been.

It's hard to step out from behind your baggage. It's risky. Anytime you put the real you out there, you risk the opportunity for rejection. The problem is that if you aren't truly known, then you aren't truly loved. Somewhere in the back of your mind, you question whether people would accept you if they truly knew you (all of you). It's true; not everyone is going to be "your people." Just look what happened when all the pomp and circumstance was over for Saul.

Read 1 Samuel 10:25-27. What happened after Saul was declared king?

Everyone went home. It all seems a little anticlimactic, doesn't it? Saul had no palace or capital city to go home to. He just walked back home—but he wasn't alone. He was surrounded by a group of valiant men. Men who had been moved in their heart to help and support him. It is impossible to lead alone.

Yet, don't miss verse 27. There were also naysayers. Of course there were. In fact, this verse says, "they despised him." There are always naysayers. Listen,

When you try to make a difference and influence others, you will always have some group of people who have something negative to say about you.

when you put yourself out there, when you risk being real and vulnerable, when you try to make a difference and influence others, you will always have some group of people who have something negative to say about you. I love what Brené Brown says, "If you're not in the arena also getting your [butt] kicked, I'm not interested in your feedback."[11] Listen, it's easy for others to criticize from the couch!

It's scary being real. A couple of years ago I was in Yuma, Arizona, speaking with the Aspire Women's Event. I was still reeling from my divorce and the fallout with my adult children was brutal. It was about an hour before the event was to start, and it was time for the VIP session. This is a time when women can come early and get to know the speakers, comedians, and worship leaders a little better. It is usually a more intimate setting than the main event. I was on the phone with one of my children who was angry at the other one about something I don't even remember now. This was just more wreckage washing up on shore. The root of this issue was deep hurt and brokenness. I have realized through much counseling that the only person I can truly control is me. And trust me, that is a full-time job! I was on the phone with adult children who were fighting about things I could not control. I finally told them in disgust, *"You work it out, because* **I have to go teach people about Jesus!"** I hung up the phone with tears welling up in my eyes, wondering what on earth I was doing teaching people about Jesus when I was such a mess myself.

As I walked out on stage and sat down in one of the four chairs, I heard my ministry friends sharing about their lives. They shared about where they were from, what God had called them to do, their long years of marriage to their wonderful husbands, and the fact that their children were walking with the Lord. Honestly, my heart was about to break. I was trying so hard to hold it together. Who was going to listen to a Bible teacher who breaks down on stage? Yet, when it got to me, I couldn't fake it any longer. I opened my mouth, and this is what came out: "Hi. I'm Mary Shannon, one of your Bible teachers tonight. I was married twenty-five years until the wheels came off, and to be quite honest, I cannot stand either one of my adult kids tonight." I then started to cry. My friend next to me wrapped her arms around me and the others on stage looked at me with such love I cannot even explain it. They knew the masks were coming off!

As I looked into the audience, tears were running down faces. To be honest, what God did in that VIP session that night was remarkable. It was as if I broke the ice. The entire event that night was so powerful, and I realized something amazing. Women are more drawn to your brokenness than to your perfection—which, by the way, is a total façade!

Just as Saul had done nothing to deserve to be king yet God chose him, I realized that night that I had done nothing to deserve my calling or spiritual gift. It was not given to me to validate my spiritual walk or to elevate me in any way. I was given a gift to use and give away to others even in times of brokenness. That is what spiritual gifts are for! If you want to evaluate your spirituality, then check your fruit. The fruit of the Spirit is evidence of your walk with God, not a life free from suffering.

Read 1 Samuel 11:1-2. What was the situation that Jabesh-gilead found themselves in?

What condition for a covenant did Nahash require? Why?

Wow, the people of Jabesh-gilead (who were Israelites) found themselves between a real rock and a hard place. Talk about a lose-lose situation. Obviously, they did not believe that if they fought the Ammonites they would prove victorious. Therefore, they offered to surrender and become their slaves. How sad, considering that four hundred years before God had freed Israel from bondage under the Egyptians. He had established them as a free nation! Yet now a part of this nation is once again facing bondage.

Nahash had isolated Jabesh-gilead, surrounding them and cutting them off. He not only wanted to enslave them but to humiliate and cripple them as well. He wanted to take their freedom and their hope. First, by gouging out their right eyes, he would glorify himself and humiliate the men of Jabesh-gilead—and, ultimately, the nation of Israel, proving this new king Saul incapable of protecting his people. Second, he would render the men unable to fight effectively in battle. They would have fought hand-to-hand combat, holding their shields in their left hands and fighting with their right hands. This would have meant that the right eye was the dominant eye peering out from behind the shield. Without the use of their right eyes, the possibility of regaining their freedom in the future would be unlikely.

I find it very interesting that the name *Nahash* means serpent or snake.[13]

Extra Insight

Scholars think that Jabesh-gilead was probably located east of the Jordan River, and about 20 miles south of the Sea of Galilee. Its name means "dry, rugged" or "dry place of Gilead."[12]

Do you see any similarities between Nahash and our enemy, Satan? List the similarities below. If you have the time, back up your thoughts with Scripture.

Does 1 Samuel 11:3 strike you as odd? Why in the world would Nahash, who had already surrounded Jabesh-gilead, allow them to wait seven days and send out a 911 message for help?

Can you say arrogance? He had to believe that no one would come and save them. Worst case scenario, his name would become well known throughout the land of Israel and he would be greatly feared. Watch out, Nahash. Pride comes before a fall! How many powerful people have fallen because of arrogance?

Read 1 Samuel 11:4-6. How did the people of Gibeah respond to the news?

Where was Saul coming from when he ran into the people? What was his response to the news?

The messengers of Jabesh-gilead went straight to Gibeah, the hometown of Saul, their new king. The fact that Saul was still working the herds in the field tells us that the "kingdom" of Israel was far from established. When Saul heard the news through the cries of the people, Scripture says that "the Spirit of God came upon Saul . . . and his anger was greatly aroused" (v. 6 NKJV).

The Hebrew word here for anger is 'aph. The definition of this word is "a nostril, nose, face, anger."[14] So, in other words, Saul's anger could be seen on his face immediately. This was not an anger he could hide. This was a righteous anger that needed action.

Read John 2:13-22. Who else had a righteous anger that needed action?

In John 2:17, what did the disciples remember?

Jesus's words caused the disciples to recall a messianic prophecy from Psalm 69, revealing that the Messiah would have zeal for God's house. The word *zeal* in John 2:17 is quite interesting in the Greek. It is *zelos*, which means "to have warmth of feeling for or against, to be zealous or jealous."[15] It is also an onomatopoeia word, which is "the formation of a word from a sound associated with what is named. In other words, the sound of the word *zeal* mimics the sound of water boiling over from the heat. The root *zeo* means to boil."[16]

Have you ever had zeal? Have you ever felt an anger that you could not keep from showing on your face? You could literally feel yourself about to boil over. If so, describe it briefly.

Yep, me too! I wish I could tell you it was always a righteous anger, but I can't. In both scenarios with Saul and Jesus, the anger was fueled by the Spirit of God. He used this fuel to bring action on behalf of those who could not defend themselves. This was the moment that Saul, the newly anointed king, would prove to his nation that he had their backs! Go get 'em, Saul!

Read 1 Samuel 11:6-8. What did Saul do to motivate the men of Israel to step up and fight for Jabesh-gilead?

Reading this is like reading *The Godfather*. Talk about waking up with a horse head in your bed. Saul is basically making them an offer they can't refuse and demanding that the people follow his lead.

How do you motivate a nation to rise up and defend an atrocity? Body parts seem to work. Today we see all kinds of atrocities. I wonder sometimes, do we need more tears or more zeal? If we would all wake up from our complacency and come together, what kinds of things could we accomplish to help the hopeless?

Read 1 Samuel 11:9-11. How did Saul lead the Israelites to victory?

Saul and his army accomplished victory over Nahash with a surprise attack early in the morning before daybreak. I guess Nahash's arrogance did not serve him well after all.

What kind of things bring out your zeal? What kinds of things are you passionate about? When you hear of the injustices in our world today, do you feel the boiling begin? Sometimes I wonder if our comfort today can hinder us from true compassion—emotion with motion. What good is emotion without legs? When was the last time you really felt a stirring in your soul to help a fellow human being without expecting anything in return? Remember, our own brokenness and vulnerability may be not only the catalyst for compassion but also the actual means for it.

Prayer Prompt

Ask God to bring to your awareness areas where He would like to use you to show compassion—areas in your community where you can make a difference and create opportunities for those who seem to be between a rock and a hard place. Ask God to keep your blessings in the forefront of your awareness and to give you the zeal to pass those blessings along to your neighbor. Don't forget to ask Him for the courage to share your own stories of brokenness so others know your actions are coming from a place of empathy and not elitism.

DAY 5

Scripture Focus

1 Samuel 11:12-15;
12:1-15

Yesterday we saw Saul lead Israel to a great victory over the Ammonites. Certain elements of this battle remind me of Israel's battle against the Midianites hundreds of years before as recorded in Judges 6–7. Let me summarize the highlights. This battle was led by a different insecure and naïve young man, Gideon. Like Saul, Gideon didn't see himself as any kind of

leader. When God approached him, he was hiding in a wine press threshing wheat. (You do realize that a wine press is not the place to thresh wheat!) He was hiding from the Midianites whose mode of oppression was to starve the nation of Israel into submission.

God showed up to this young man and called him a "mighty warrior" (Judges 6:12 NIV). Isn't it amazing that God sees our future potential and not just our current posture? Gideon eventually defeated the massive army of Midian using three hundred men broken into three groups. They surprised the Midianites during the morning watch, or in the middle of the night. This ragtag group of renegades defeated the enormous, well-trained army of Midian.

So, with similar tactics, Saul took the volunteer army of Israel and defeated the professional armies of Nahash.

I love stories! Stories passed down through generations preserving years of ancient history. History teaches us about our human origins, our struggles, and our achievements. Within the pages of history, we find universal truths and repetitive themes hidden in different times and cultures. When we hear a story, we naturally identify with one or more of its characters, allowing them to teach us long after they have passed.

Isn't this what happens when we study the Bible? I wonder if one of Saul's valiant men had reminded him of young Gideon one night when he was feeling especially insecure. I can't tell you how many times I used the story of David to inspire my own young man. Saul seems to be learning from some of the great leaders of the past. It's often said that imitation is the highest form of flattery.

Read 1 Samuel 11:12-13. What do the people want to do after their victory over the Ammonites, and what is Saul's response?

People never cease to amaze me. After this amazing victory, before the Israelites can even celebrate, they decide to go on a witch hunt for the former naysayers. What? Haven't enough people died? Their young king, Saul, has just experienced his first victory—and probably his first battle ever—and instead of celebrating as a newly united nation, they want to turn on each other. They think the best gift they can give their king is to assassinate the ones who didn't "vote" for him. They fought for freedom, but now they are actually going to take it away. Holy identity politics, Batman!

Extra Insight

Reading the Bible is a non-negotiable for our spiritual growth, but I encourage you to expand your reading list. Find a biography or novel about an inspirational woman who impacted her culture. She may have lived long before you were born, but I imagine she has much to teach you.

Does the underlying "us versus them" construct sound familiar? Talk about universal repetitive themes. Be careful: often our enemy will not beat us using a full-frontal attack but instead will infiltrate and divide. Thank goodness Saul has the wisdom to put an end to this. This is not a time for division but unity.

> **Read 1 Samuel 11:14-15. If Saul has already been anointed as king, what does it mean when it says they made Saul king in Gilgal?**

Listen, it's one thing to be anointed or appointed, but it's another to have the nation united behind you. We know that initially, there were those who doubted Saul. But now the proof is in the pudding. The evidence is in the doing. Some people had asked, "How can this man save us?" and Saul has now given them the answer! Swoosh! Nothing but net! Drop the mic!

> **Read 1 Samuel 12:1-5. Spend some time meditating on all that the prophet Samuel has been through with the nation of Israel, and consider his feelings regarding Israel's request for a king. Write your insights below.**

> **Have you ever been in a situation where you believed that you were completely faithful in your calling and yet, ultimately, you were rejected? Have you ever felt unappreciated for your sacrifices? If so, were you able to voice those feelings without appearing boastful or praise hungry? Explain.**

Is it just me, or do you also feel pain beneath the words of Samuel? He had given his life serving the nation of Israel, and they thanked him by asking for a king. In many ways, Samuel can understand the rejection God felt as a result of Israel's unfaithfulness. I think this might be what God was trying to show Samuel—He was essentially saying to him through this situation, "Samuel, I know you are feeling rejected, and I know how bad it hurts. Trust me, I know! But Samuel, ultimately, you are just the middleman, remember? They are actually rejecting Me!"

So, Samuel stood up in front of them and made his farewell address, his retirement speech. Do you think Samuel could relate to the police officer or doctor or any dedicated worker who gives his or her whole life to their duty and in the end gets the symbolic gold watch?

Samuel realized that his role, in its entirety, was no longer needed. Much like John the Baptist, he knew it was time for him to become less and for someone else to become more (John 3:30). Israel had the king they had longed for, and all seemed to be going as planned, but Samuel had some final words they needed to hear.

He began by saying (my paraphrase), "I know I am old and that my sons do not reflect my ways, but please, before I address you for the last time, tell me if there is anything about me that will cause you to doubt my words?" The people respond, "No, you've never exploited or taken advantage of us. You've never abused us or lined your own pockets."

Things had not gone as Samuel had hoped. His sons were not on stage with him, but instead were in the audience. (I am sure he felt much guilt about that.) The nation that he had led all of his life had ignored his advice, and they now had a king. I wonder if he had any moments of doubt, questioning if anything he had done really mattered. Yet here at this moment, he had to put aside his own emotions, his own personal hurt, and bring the Israelites the message they so desperately need to hear. He must not make his words about him. His job was to bring the words of God.

Now that he had settled any case against himself, he began by laying out their case before God.

Read 1 Samuel 12:6-15, taking time to walk through the facts of this case.

Why was Samuel making this case? (v. 7)

What stories or evidence did he use to make this case? List below all of the people Samuel named whom God sent to deliver His people.

What was Samuel's overall point?

If we do not recognize our patterns and do the healing work, a new king, new job, new marriage, or new town will not prevent us from repeating them.

Basically, Samuel was showing them the patterns of behavior that had been grooved into their tribes for generations. He wanted them to recognize that these patterns of unfaithfulness didn't just exist in their past but were evident in their present; and if they weren't careful, these patterns would destroy their future. Looking back in this way is important because recognition is the first step to healing. If you can't recognize your sinful patterns, you can't turn away from them, and Samuel wanted them to break the cycle!

The people believed this new king would give them the outcome they desired. Samuel was trying to tell them that with or without a king, true freedom is found in God. Ultimately, God was still in control. He was still on the throne. If Saul did not seek the heart of God and lead the people in His ways, the cycle of bondage would continue with or without a king.

I can empathize with Samuel in this story. If you have ever felt rejected, you know how painful it can be, especially if you feel like you have given your all to the other person or organization. If not dealt with correctly, rejection can breed all sorts of unhealthy emotions. While Samuel had his own issues to deal with, he remained faithful by warning the Israelites to deal with theirs. If we do not recognize our patterns and do the healing work, a new king, new job, new marriage, or new town will not prevent us from repeating them.

Prayer Prompt

As you spend time with the Father today, ask Him to pour His love into your rejection wound. Remember, God will never leave us or reject us. He has entered into a covenant relationship with us that is held together by His own righteousness. Ask Him to help you forgive those who have injured you. I find it helpful to remind myself of all the ways God has forgiven me. Also ask God to reveal to you any patterns that are keeping you stuck. Though this can be painful, it's necessary. Relocating or remodeling will not help until the foundation is repaired.

Video Viewer Guide: Week 2

Often _____ or _____ can be great revealers of our lack of trust and self-control.

When we grumble, complain, and judge, we not only _____ such behaviors, we _____ them.

What God really wanted was their _____.

_____ always comes before healing.

The danger of an image is that the object may easily become confused with what it was intended only to _____.

Without the presence of the _____, there is no true power—just an empty, lifeless _____.

We will only trust God to the extent that we recognize His unbelievable _____ for us.

Scriptures: Numbers 21:4-9, John 3:14, 2 Corinthians 5:21, Genesis 1:26, 1 Samuel 12

Week 3

Oh, No!
Now I'm Losing Control

Recognizing Our Helplessness

1 Samuel 13–16

DAY 1

At the end of last week, we saw Samuel move past his own personal hurt and speak truth to the people, reminding them of God's repetitive deliverance and urging them to follow Him faithfully. It takes a lot to swallow our own pain and disappointment and filter our words through the grace of God. Sometimes it seems to leave our tongues bleeding from all the biting. I wonder if Samuel had a little blood in his mouth that day. There have been many days I've had to clamp down hard on my ole tongue.

In Matthew 12:34, Jesus tells us that "out of the abundance of the heart the mouth speaks." Jesus spoke only the words the Father gave Him. The love reigning in His heart was evident in what came out of His mouth. His heart showed that sometimes love requires speaking the hard message, sometimes love requires careful word selection, and sometimes love requires silence. Words are powerful!

Read Proverbs 18:21 in the margin. Do your words reveal your love for others or just your love to talk? How have you used your words this week?

Scripture Focus

1 Samuel 12:16-25;
1 Samuel 13:1-7

*The tongue can bring death or life;
  those who love to talk will reap the consequences.
    (Proverbs 18:21 NLT)*

Samuel moved past his personal feelings and faithfully spoke words of both rebuke and hope. He warned the people to stop walking in the sinful trenches that the generations before them had dug. He challenged them to break the patterns of the past, letting them know that it was not too late to repent.

Today we too have a choice of how we will respond. Past failures do not destroy today's free will. We must not let the past *define* us but, instead, let it *develop* us!

Words are powerful, but sometimes they need an added punch to sink in. In this scenario, God brought the punch.

Read 1 Samuel 12:16-18. In order to get the people's attention, what did Samuel ask of the Lord? (v. 17)

To me, this seems like God was flexing His omnipotent arm through a very unseasonable weather occurrence. Enough to scare the crud out of them! This would be like Samuel calling down snow in Phoenix, Arizona, in the middle of the 110-degree summer. You may remember that the disciples had a similar response when Jesus calmed the wind and the waves (Mark 4:35-41). Let's be honest, "mother nature" is a force to be reckoned with. Could this be why they call her "*mother* nature"? Because as the saying goes, "When mama ain't happy, ain't nobody happy!" When mama is raging, you best run for cover.

It doesn't take a brain surgeon to know that the only one who can control creation is the One who created it. When the Creator speaks, creation must obey, and it was evident to the nation of Israel that God spoke that day.

My question is, *Why did God choose to respond like this now? Why did He not flex His muscle when they first asked for a king?*

I truly have no idea, but if you allow me to speculate, I can make some suggestions. Maybe if Samuel had brought this sign earlier, they would have changed their minds momentarily about having a man as a king; but what good would that have been in the long run? When the thunder of restraint passed, wouldn't they have just ended up here again still fighting for control?

Could it be that sometimes we have to live out the consequences of our choices in order to learn and grow? Sometimes we don't feel the fear and gravity of our choices until years down the road. Sometimes it takes thunder and lightning to wake us from our insane stupors and force us to take a long look at what life is like when we insist on being in control. This wasn't the thunder of restraint. It was the thunder of revelation.

That moment of revelation is when the true journey begins. The thought of continuing down the same road scares us more than stopping to address what got us here in the first place. Self-work can be very painful, but it is worth it. We have to fight feelings of shame, regret, and even despair. We have to face questions such as, *What can I do about it now, when the damage is already done?*

Oh, sister! All is not lost. Because of the grace of God, His mercies are new every morning! Remember, life is not about outcomes but about process.

God is molding you into the masterpiece He knows you are. There is nothing He cannot use for your good and His glory if we allow Him.

Is the thunder roaring in your life? Have fear and anxiety convinced you there is no hope for you? Do you feel like you have fallen too far? When you are around other Christian women, do you feel like the broken one?

Girlfriend, we all are the broken one! We have a God who is willing to enter into those wounds with His healing salve. If you are looking for perfection, you will not find it in the people of Scripture, nor will you find it in the author of this study. What you will find are the testimonies of people just like you, people who are trying to navigate this fallen world by holding on for dear life to Jesus, the only perfect One!

What do the verses below tell us about God's desire for us?

⁴For everything that was written in the past was written to teach us, so that through the endurance taught in the Scriptures and the encouragement they provide we might have hope.

⁵May the God who gives endurance and encouragement give you the same attitude of mind toward each other that Christ Jesus had, ⁶so that with one mind and one voice you may glorify the God and Father of our Lord Jesus Christ.

(Romans 15:4-6 NIV)

God does not withhold Himself from you in times of trouble; He runs to you. Everything in Scripture was written to say, "Keep going, girl. Stick with it." Navigating this world takes endurance and, most of all, encouragement from others who have experienced similar struggles. Our hope is not found in our accomplishments but in Jesus Christ, who accomplished our salvation on the cross. He is our living hope. This is the encouragement of the Scriptures, and this is the encouragement we are to share with the world around us—all doing our part to become a choir with many voices and many stories, all harmonizing together to glorify the Lord Jesus Christ.

So, praise God in the storm. Sometimes it is exactly what we need in order to wake up and go a different direction.

Samuel told the people, "Do not fear. You have done all this wickedness; yet do not turn aside from following the LORD, but serve the LORD with all of

Learn from where you have been. Now, look forward, because that is where we are going.

your heart" (1 Samuel 12:20 NKJV). He was telling them, "Learn from where you have been. Now, look forward, because that is where we are going."

Samuel had to say the same to himself. In verse 23, he acknowledged that if he didn't continue to pray for this nation, he was no better than they were. He too had a choice to get over his own hurt and move forward!

Now this is where it gets interesting.

Read 1 Samuel 13:1-4. What happens here?

Saul had handled the great threat coming from the east, the Ammonites, but now—a number of years later—he must deal with the threat that has once again risen from the west, the Philistines. Somehow, this nation had pushed their way back into the territories of Israel. I am sure they had used both power and persuasion. The threat of Philistine military force was something most people wanted to avoid at all costs, and as long as the Israelites minded their own business and paid taxes to the Philistines,[2] they could stave off conflict. (Oh, the Israelites' tendency to settle!)

But now, Saul was organizing an army. Three thousand men were being professionally trained by Saul and his grown son, Jonathan, at two north-south military strongholds (1 Samuel 13:2). We are not sure what started the fight between Jonathan and the Philistine garrison at Geba, but we know that Israel became "obnoxious to the Philistines" (13:4 NIV), or as another translation puts it, "a stench to the Philistines" (ESV). Had Jonathan refused to submit to the Philistine's stick (their force) or to accept their carrot (submit and live in peace)? Did Jonathan instigate a fight? I don't know, but war was brewing!

What I notice in this story is that as Saul began to organize and train his troops to defend the nation, there was massive pushback. Whether they instigated this conflict or not, the Israelites were not called to settle among the Philistines and allow the Philistines to subdue them.

Are there any areas in your life where you are settling? If so, are you settling out of fear or comfort? Explain.

Have you ever noticed that just when we begin to move forward and make progress, creating positive change or establishing healthy boundaries, the change seems to cause more chaos at first? It's one thing to recognize unhealthy patterns, but it's another thing to start changing them. It's one thing to recognize enemy strongholds in your territory, and it's another thing to remove them. When we commit to progress, often it gets worse before it gets better. Like cleaning out your closet or garage, you've got to pull stuff out and mess stuff up before real, lasting change can take place.

When you commit to progress, you'd better expect pushback! When you begin working out, you better expect the pain of sore muscles. I've been so sore from working out at times that I couldn't even sit on the toilet. My first thought is always, *Why am I doing this*? In our financial life, it seems like the minute we begin to establish a budget and commit to hold to it, everything in the house breaks. Likewise, in our emotional lives, cleaning house can be painful. It can seem overwhelming to heal old wounds and traumas. It can be even harder setting healthy boundaries with those around us because they are used to our old dance moves. Any time we change our steps, they will not know what to do and, trust me, they won't like it.

When any kind of pushback happens, our tendency is to stop fighting and settle.

Read 1 Samuel 13:5-7. What did the men of Israel do when they realized they were in trouble?

The Israelites ran and hid in "caves and in holes and in rocks and in tombs and in cisterns" (v. 6) instead of trusting God and standing up to their enemy. They were willing to give the enemy a foothold in their land instead of doing the work to cast them out. It's tempting to run from conflict in our lives, but the only way we will stay in the fight is if our "why" is big enough. Let me ask you: How badly do you want to be free? Are you willing to risk comfort for freedom?

When you decide to make progress or grow, expect pushback. But just remember, if you are not growing, you are dying. You're either moving forward or backward. If you're not careful, one day you will wake up and the very enemy you once pushed out will be back with garrisons in your land. It's then that you need to look that old enemy in the eyes.

The first step to solving any problem is to acknowledge it. Then, ask yourself, "How did I end up back here?" I am sure you will discover that it

When you decide to make progress or grow, expect pushback.

was one tiny step of compromise at a time. That's the thing about patterns: we gravitate toward old ruts. Now, embrace this new opportunity for victory, acknowledging there is still something you need to learn in this area of your life.

Prayer Prompt

Spend some time journaling today. What battle are you currently fighting? Have you been here before—not just similar circumstances, but similar people or feelings as well? Now ask your Father to show you what this battle is actually about, bringing anything hidden into the light. Ask Him to reveal any patterns that have brought you back to this place—choices, wounds, vulnerabilities, relationships, and fears. You may be tempted to run and hide, but *don't give in*. Ask God for the courage to stand with Him to face the true enemy. Remember, you are completely safe with your Father!

DAY 2

Scripture Focus

1 Samuel 13:8-14

As we saw yesterday, quite some time has passed between chapters 12 and 13. In chapter 12, Saul seems to be a fairly young man. His kingship is new. He has proven very successful as a leader, and the nation of Israel has united under his reign. But in chapter 13, Saul has a grown son, Jonathan, who is quite the warrior in Saul's army. We read yesterday that it is Jonathan who draws first blood with the Philistine army (13:3), and we can only assume that happened under the complete authority of his father.

We only have certain highlights from Saul's reign, probably because the author of 1 and 2 Samuel wrote this book during the period of the Divided Kingdom,[3] and his emphasis was David, Israel's beloved king. Therefore, we do our best with limited information to put the pieces of the puzzle together in order to better understand this man, Saul.

Jonathan had drawn first blood, and now both armies had assembled for war—the Philistines at Michmash and the Israelites at Gilgal. Remember, the land of Israel is very small. The distance between these two strategic high places was roughly 12–15 miles,[4] so one could see across the stretch of land. It was not unusual for the armies to have a full view of each other across the valleys between them. When the Israelites saw how outnumbered they were by the Philistines, they freaked out.

Don't forget that the Philistines were one of the first people to enter into the Iron Age, so their weaponry was much more advanced than the Israelites.[5] (Actually, later we read in 1 Samuel 13:19-22 that the only Israelite men who were equipped with weapons at all were Saul and Jonathan.) The fear proved too much for the Israelite army. They began to desert en masse. They ran for cover. They hid in caves and cisterns. Many escaped across the Jordan River, taking refuge in the cities of Gad and Gilead.

Before we pick up with our reading for today, let's look again at how our reading ended yesterday.

Read 1 Samuel 13:7b in the margin. What does it say about Saul?

Saul remained at Gilgal, and all the troops with him were quaking with fear.
(1 Samuel 13:7b NIV)

If someone told me that my king held his ground despite his own fear, I would consider him a strong leader. Now, this is where it gets interesting—or maybe confusing!

Write 1 Samuel 13:8 below.

There are those who want to connect 1 Samuel 10:8, where Samuel tells Saul to wait for him seven days at Gilgal, with 1 Samuel 13:8, where we read that Saul waited seven days without any sign of Samuel.[6] I do not see this connection. It doesn't seem to make any sense to me in the chronology of the story—considering that in chapter 10, Saul is a young man being anointed, while in chapter 13 he has a grown son. Either way, what we do know is that there was an agreed upon time for Saul to wait for Samuel to come, seven days. As the high priest, Samuel would have been the one to inquire of God, asking for His protection on the nation of Israel. He would have done this through offering a sacrifice.

According to verse 8, how long did Saul wait?

It seems to me that Saul did exactly what Samuel had asked. If anyone missed the appointment, it wasn't Saul. The verse is clear that Samuel did not show up at the appointed time. I would love to know why, but we are not given one ounce of explanation.

Describe below what you think the atmosphere might have been like for Saul while he waited those seven days.

I don't think "tense" quite covers it. He was losing soldiers every day, and I can imagine the pressure he was getting from his commanders. "Saul, do something! If we wait any longer, we won't have an army to fight with! Why is Samuel not here? He may have been killed on his way. You are our king! You need to do something!"

Having waited the seven days, Saul decided to take charge and move forward. What was he supposed to do? Samuel was a "no show." Isn't that what leaders are paid the big bucks to do? Therefore, he proceeded with the offerings without Samuel. This part gets a little sticky for me. I wonder if Saul actually performed the offerings himself or if Ahijah did. Let me be clear. If he did, he clearly overstepped his authority and disobeyed the law of God.[7] Yet in the very next chapter, we see that Ahijah the priest, who was in charge of the ephod, was with Saul in battle (14:3). Saul actually asked Ahijah to "bring the ark of God here" (v. 18), symbolizing his desire for them to inquire of God regarding the battle. Therefore, is there a possibility that the author credited Saul with actually performing the offering when, in reality, he just approved it by proceeding with another priest like Ahijah? If Ahijai was there, would Saul have performed the offering? I don't know! What I do know is the next part seems very peculiar to me.

> **What feeling do you get when you read 1 Samuel 13:10? What do you notice about the timing?**

Could this possibly be read as entrapment? This is my opinion, but it's as if Samuel was hiding in the bushes waiting for Saul to screw up and then pounce. As soon as Saul had performed the sacrifices—*bam!*—Samuel jumped out and said, "What have you done?" (v. 11).

> **Read 1 Samuel 13:11-12. What was Saul's response? Do you find his explanation reasonable? Why or why not?**

Extra Insight

The ark of the covenant was a symbol of the presence and glory of God. Inside it were placed the tables of testimony (Ten Commandments), a pot of manna, and Aaron's rod. It was called the ark of God (1 Samuel 3:3); the ark of God's strength (2 Chronicles 6:41); the ark of the covenant of the Lord (Numbers 10:33); and the ark of the testimony (Exodus 30:6).[8]

I can understand Saul's logic. He laid out the facts as he knew them: "I was losing my soldiers by the day, pressure was mounting, you were a no-show, the Philistines were ready to attack, and I had not sought the help of the Lord."

I am curious. What would you have done in that situation? Describe a time in your life when you felt incredible pressure to make a decision. What was the outcome?

Much about this story baffles me, but especially Samuel's pronouncement to Saul.

Summarize 1 Samuel 13:13-14 below in your own words.

Samuel told Saul that what he had done was foolish, and that if he had not made this mistake, God would have established his kingdom forever. But now Saul's kingdom would be taken away by another whom God had already been looking for.

With the weight of the nation on his shoulders and facing an impossible situation, Saul had made the choice to proceed to war without Samuel. It is in this moment that I wish I knew more of the story between chapter 12 and chapter 13. Had Saul leaned on Samuel for years? Had Samuel, who had devoted his life to leading Israel, mentored Saul? Who knew the nation better than Samuel? Could Samuel have taken this personally, if old rejection wounds were triggered? More importantly, what did the words of Samuel do to Saul when he said, "You have done foolishly"? Remember, Saul was the beloved son of a powerful man, no doubt seeking to please his father. Had Samuel become a father figure to him? Was Samuel's disappointment devastating to the psyche of Saul?

On Day 1 of this week, we discussed how powerful words can be. Do you ever hear words of disappointment from the past ringing in your head—possibly from someone you admired? If so, describe how they make you feel.

Are there still times when you are subconsciously trying to prove those words wrong? If so, write about it briefly.

I also struggle with the fact that Samuel told Saul that if he hadn't made this one mistake, God would have established his kingdom *forever*. I find this questionable in light of Genesis 49:10.

Read Genesis 49:10 in the margin. What does it say about the scepter?

The scepter will not depart from Judah, nor the ruler's staff from between his feet, until he to whom it belongs shall come and the obedience of the nations shall be his.
(Genesis 49:10 NIV)

This prophecy would be fulfilled in the eternal kingship of Jesus Christ, who was the son of David from the tribe of Judah, not the tribe of Benjamin, which was Saul's tribe. Therefore, Saul's kingdom could not have been established *forever*.

The Message says it this way: "If you had kept the appointment that your GOD commanded, by now GOD would have set a firm and lasting foundation under your kingly rule over Israel. As it is, your kingly rule is already falling to pieces. GOD is out looking for your replacement right now" (1 Samuel 13:13-14 MSG). Notice that *The Message's* author, Eugene Peterson, did not use the words "forever" or "eternal" in his paraphrase.

Perhaps Samuel was simply saying that Saul's kingdom would have remained intact to be passed down to Jonathan.

Without considering any prior stories about Saul, does Samuel's statement seem harsh to you? Explain your response.

I realize that without more information, we may not be aware of an evident decline in the character of Saul, but I cannot help thinking that Samuel's statement seems harsh. In light of the grace God showed Eli, Hophni, and Phinehas, this judgment seems swift. God allowed the scorning of His offerings to go on a long time before there were consequences for the house of Eli. Yet, Saul was in a life or death situation, but there seemed to be no grace. I also find it interesting that the words "thus sayeth the Lord" seem to be missing from the entire discourse.

Although I do not have all of the specifics for this story (and actually have more questions), I truly believe that this experience changed Saul in a dramatic way. After chapter 13, the personality and behaviors of Saul seem to become erratic. It is the beginning of a slow decline that will end in torment. I can't help but wonder what this event from chapter 13 did to begin the descent. What did these "once and done" words of Samuel do to Saul? "You've failed and there is no way back!" Saul gave no response to Samuel's words. He just moved on as if they had never been said. But they *were* said, and I believe they became the seeds that began his paranoia. From here on out, we see Saul desperately grasping for control when, in reality, he was losing it.

Of course, we can never understand all that goes on inside another person. I can barely understand what is going on inside of *me*! When I take time to explore my own childhood, I wonder if I am even remembering it accurately. I am definitely remembering it from the perspective of a child. Sometimes it can be just as difficult to understand narratives in Scripture like this one. But whether intentional or unintentional, accurate or inaccurate, we all have moments and words that have marked us, like Saul. And we all need God's help in determining how to respond to them.

Prayer Prompt

Ask your Father to reveal the moments, events, or words that have marked you. Whose words seem to be on repeat in your head? Are you allowing these sound bites from the past to affect your present? What are you trying to prove

> We all have moments and words that have marked us. And we all need God's help in determining how to respond to them.

and to whom are you trying to prove it? How do these things relate to the issue of control in your life? Ask God to show you what you need to own and what you need to let go of.

DAY 3

Scripture Focus

1 Samuel 13:15-23; 14:1-52

As we resume our story today, we will see what happens after Samuel's dramatic announcement that Saul's kingdom will not continue and that God will replace him with "a man after his own heart" (1 Samuel 13:14). During the next sequence of events, I want you to notice all of the actions, non-actions, and reactions of Saul. Along the way I will give you opportunities to write down your insights and observations. Let's dive in!

Read 1 Samuel 13:15-23. What did the people of Israel not have, and how did they compensate?

Extra Insight

The name *Jonathan* means "Jehovah has given."[9]

After Samuel confronted Saul, he went home while Saul went into battle, taking his troops to Geba and joining his son Jonathan. The Philistine army started to make their move to flank the nation of Israel, cutting off any escape routes.

Now read 1 Samuel 14:1-3a. While Jonathan was engaging the enemy, where was Saul?

Why do you think Jonathan did not tell his father what he was doing?

Once again, we see the bravery of Jonathan as he and his armor-bearer climbed through the great crevasse separating the two armies to engage the enemy. At this point, Saul was camped at the outskirts of Gibeah in a cave with his six hundred men (v. 2). This is a good place to stop and write your first insights about Saul. Consider his lack of movement. Remember, the Philistines were on the move and had sent out three regimens along the main roadways surrounding Geba (also known as Gibeah).

Why do you think Saul was not preparing for battle? Might he have been apprehensive to fight? What kinds of things might he have been thinking about?

Now read 1 Samuel 14:3b-15. Using the space provided below, draw a picture or create an outline of how this story unfolds.

As the story continues, we see that one of Saul's watchmen saw the fighting going on in Michmash. Verse 15 states that "there was a panic in the camp [of the Philistines], in the field, and among all of the people. The garrison and even the raiders trembled, the earth quaked, and it became a very great panic." This caught the watchful eye of Saul's spies, and they reported it to Saul.

Saul had no idea who was fighting or who started it. He had his men take a roll call to see who might be missing from his army and, therefore, responsible for this attack. Lo and behold, it was his own son Jonathan (v. 17). Saul had no idea Jonathan and his armor-bearer had climbed through the crevasse.

Do you find it interesting that once again Jonathan was the first to engage in battle—and Saul didn't know? Where do you think Saul's head was right then?

Read 1 Samuel 14:18. Saul immediately called for Ahijah the priest to bring the ark which, as we saw yesterday, symbolized inquiring of God regarding their engagement in the battle. Why do you think he was calling upon the priest to decide?

In the next verses, we see that before the priest could even throw out the Urim and the Thummim, Saul stopped the priest and joined in the fight (vv. 19-20). It's almost as if he thought, "What the heck am I doing? The battle has already started!"

Why do you think Saul would inquire of the priest and then not wait for the answer?

Why do you think that suddenly Saul couldn't seem to make a decision? Was he just trying to walk through the religious motions? If so, why and for whom?

What other questions do you have about what was happening?

There was great confusion among the Philistines, and all the men of Israel who had been hiding came to join in the battle (vv. 20-22). In verse 23 we read that "the LORD saved Israel that day." With momentum on their side, an emotional Saul made a vow.

Read 1 Samuel 14:24-46. What vow did Saul make that set off all of this drama?

Saul called for a fast, forbidding his soldiers from eating anything until they had completely annihilated his enemy. As a result of this oath, Saul caused his soldiers to sin. They were so famished that they began to take the spoils and failed to prepare the meat properly, breaking the dietary laws. Jonathan, not being present when the oath was made, ate some honey during the battle, and Saul nearly put his own son to death!

According to verse 24, how did Saul refer to the Philistines?

Do you think he was taking this battle personally? Explain.

Does his oath seem smart to you? Why or why not?

Read verses 29-30. What did Jonathan think of his dad's vow?

What do you think about Saul actually being prepared to kill his own son (v. 44)? What could he have been trying to prove by putting his own son to death?

Do you think he possibly might have been identifying himself with Abraham, and if so, why? Record your insights below.

Do not miss the fact that right in the middle of their battle, God had provided the very thing they needed to boost their energy: honey. It was literally pouring out before them. It was a gift from God—the very thing they needed to brighten their eyes and give them strength to keep fighting. Yet Saul would not allow them to enjoy this gift, but instead had bound them up with restriction, which later proved to be destructive when the troops sinned against God by eating a blood-drenched buffet (1 Samuel 14:31-33).

God is a God of freedom! Failing to recognize this was often the problem in ancient times, and it's often the problem today. Why do we have all of the rules we have? Are we attempting to control the flesh with outward obedience, or are we allowing God to come in and change the heart? Isn't obedience actually motivated by love? After all, Jesus said, "If you love me, you will keep my commandments" (John 14:15).

What the heck was happening to Saul, then? At the beginning of chapter 13, he seemed to be stable, holding his ground despite his fears, and preparing his soldiers for battle. He waited for Samuel, enduring the great pressure around him. But when the words of Samuel came to him, proclaiming his foolishness and the end of his kingdom, it's as though something in him snapped. Here in chapter 14, he seems apprehensive, indecisive, impulsive, and pious.

Are you sensing the emotional rollercoaster Saul was on? He was *reacting* instead of *leading*.

What do you think Saul was trying to prove with his actions in chapter 14, and to whom was he trying to prove it? What core feelings or fears do you think were going on in Saul that produced these reactionary behaviors?

What happens to *you* when you worry about what other people think?

How might this people-pleasing breed fear of failure?

How is the fear of failure connected to the fear of losing control?

Which fears cripple you? Place a check mark by the one(s) you wrestle with. Then next to each, write where that fear shows up in your life.

___ Fear of what people think

___ Fear of failure

___ Fear of losing control

Fear is an interesting thing. On the one hand, it can make us apprehensive and unable to make decisions, and on the other hand, it can make us impulsive with our decisions as we grasp for control.

Can you think of a time in your life when the fear of failure or the fear of what others would think caused you to be either reluctant or impulsive? Describe that time.

What fears might be causing you to be overly passive or overly involved in certain situations?

If you are a parent (or another kind of leader), do you find yourself reacting or controlling more than leading? What is actually lurking beneath the surface?

Fear can make us apprehensive and unable to make decisions, and on the other hand, it can make us impulsive with our decisions as we grasp for control.

Start to identify your underlying fears. Think of a couple of situations that have exposed your fears. For each situation, ask yourself what you are afraid of, and then ask yourself why. Keep asking why until you have revealed the core your underlying fear.

Situation #1:

Situation #2:

There were so many times in my twenty-five years of marriage when I, like Saul, retreated to the cave. Often haunted by personal failures, I felt insecure and inadequate. I knew the enemy was on the move. I saw the signs. Yet after years of battling, nothing seemed to change, so I continued to retreat to my cave to survive. I pledged to "die to self" and take one for the team. I was often in a secret cave of depression, but at least I was still in the marriage.

Now I see that this martyr mentality was a cop-out. It was my way of protecting myself. Don't get me wrong; I was staying in the marriage because I believed it was the right thing to do. I wanted my family together no matter what! On my own, I never would have gotten out of it. Truly I did not know what to do without injuring my children and risking religious scrutiny. The fear of both scenarios paralyzed me. I was determined to hang on to the appearance rather than work on the reality. There were plenty of things I could have done if I hadn't been so afraid that people would think less of me, that I would lose some position, or that I might appear to be a failure. The fear of appearing imperfect was too much to risk, so retreating to the cave became the norm.

I chose to give up and disengage in my marriage because I no longer saw the potential for success. Yet in my parenting, I went full bore. It's almost as if I couldn't control one, so I was dang well going to control the other.

In this quest to be the perfect mom—to prove successful somewhere—I often controlled too much. I now can see areas where I was too restrictive and did not allow myself or others to eat the eye-brightening honey. I could not have imagined putting my children to death. (Well, on most days!) But there were times when my pride and stubbornness injured my relationships with them. I wasn't willing to kill them, but sometimes I murdered their

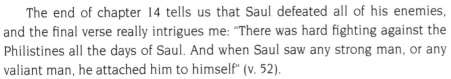

attempts to talk to me by refusing to listen, all because humility seemed like losing control, and it scared me.

In what areas of your life do you feel out of control? Are you overcompensating in other areas? If so, what are they?

The end of chapter 14 tells us that Saul defeated all of his enemies, and the final verse really intrigues me: "There was hard fighting against the Philistines all the days of Saul. And when Saul saw any strong man, or any valiant man, he attached him to himself" (v. 52).

In light of all we know about Saul's situation and psyche, why do you think he did this? I mean, obviously it was smart for a king to surround himself with valiant men. Any king would like to fill his leadership positions with the absolute cream of the crop. But I wonder if he also was trying to neutralize any potential competition. You know, "keep your friends close but your enemies closer" kind of thing.

Saul was so preoccupied with looking for potential threats that he was completely unaware of the most dangerous threat: the monster growing within him. This monster has many names, some of which are insecurity, envy, jealousy, pride, and paranoia. I'd like to leave you with this question to ponder: *How often do we, like Saul, focus on the people and circumstances in our lives while ignoring the only one we can truly change—ourselves?*

Prayer Prompt

Spend some quiet time with your Father now, asking Him to help you shift your focus from external threats to internal threats. Rather than identifying what needs to change in your exterior life, ask God to show you what needs to change in your interior life—your thoughts, feelings, and attitudes.

DAY 4

Today we will see Saul's downward spiral continue. While chapters 13–14 gave us room for speculation about his internal state, chapter 15 will not. The story itself may prove complicated, but the lesson for us will be plain as we witness Saul disobeying a direct command from God.

Scripture Focus

1 Samuel 15

Read 1 Samuel 15. What questions do you have after reading this story? In the question mark below, jot down the questions you have.

This is a difficult story, and it will be helpful for us to have some context regarding who the Amalekites were.

Read the following Scriptures, and note below any information you gather regarding the Amalekites.

Genesis 36:12, 15-16

Deuteronomy 25:17-19

Judges 6:3; 7:12

The Amalekites were the perpetual enemies of Israel. They were actually distant cousins of the Israelites, having descended from Esau. They were the first people to attack God's nation on their way from Mount Sinai to the Promised Land. In Exodus 17:8, it says that Amalek "came" and fought with Israel at Rephidim. That word in the Hebrew is bow'.[10] It can also be interpreted as "bring against" or "attack." The nation of Israel did not pass through the territory of Amalek; rather, Amalek intentionally went out of their way to attack Israel.

Not only did the Amalekites attack the Israelites, but they attacked from the rear, starting with the weak, young, old, and sick. The story of Exodus 17 tells us that God rescued the Israelites, and it states that He would not forget. He would indeed utterly blot out the Amalekites (Exodus 17:14). This is a difficult story that we want to handle carefully, so stick with me.

First, I want us to look at a couple of New Testament passages, including the teachings of Jesus.

Read Romans 12:18-20. Whose job is it to repay evil?

What command are we given regarding how to treat our enemies?

Hebrews 4:12-13 (NIV) tells us, "For the word of God is living and active. Sharper than any double-edged sword, it penetrates even to dividing soul and spirit, joints and marrow; it judges the thoughts and attitudes of the heart. Nothing in all creation is hidden from God's sight. Everything is uncovered and laid bare before the eyes of him to whom we must give account." In light of these verses, I am so glad that God is the judge and I am not.

God is the only righteous judge, considering everything is laid bare before His eyes. Since we do not share that ability with God, Romans 12 instructs us to return evil with good by meeting our enemy's needs. Yet, I do have to admit that at times the vision of the scorching hot coals mentioned here serves as my motivation to show kindness. Am I just awful? Just keeping it real, girlfriend!

Some scholars suggest that this was not a war of conquest or a war for territory or freedom but a war of justice,[11] especially in light of what God said to Moses in Deuteronomy 25:19: "Therefore when the LORD your God has given you rest from all your enemies around you, in the land that the LORD your God is giving you for an inheritance to possess, you shall blot out the memory of Amalek from under heaven; you shall not forget."

God told Saul to take no prisoners and leave the wealth behind. The goal of the attack was not to make Saul rich or increase his kingdom, but to execute justice on a rebellious group of people, the Amalekites.

At other times in the Old Testament, God seems to use the invasion of foreign nations to bring judgment on Israel as well as other nations.[12] Sadly, misguided Christians and other religious groups have adopted this pattern of thinking, trying to bring about God's kingdom or will (as they might define it) through violence or coercion. The truth is that God loves, and always has loved, *all* people. We see this love even in His covenant with the nation of Israel through whom He brought His light to the world and blessing *all nations* through the coming of the Messiah, Jesus.

The important point I want to emphasize is that our God is both just and loving, as we see throughout the Scriptures. And Jesus, the complete and perfect representation of God, taught us how we are to treat our enemies.

Spend some time meditating on the following verses. Jot down in the space provided how they speak to the love and/or justice of God.

Matthew 5:43-48

Matthew 28:18-20

Ephesians 5:1-9

Ephesians 6:10-18

Now, recall Deuteronomy 25:19, which states the Lord will "blot out" the memory of Amalek. That phrase "blot out" is the Hebrew word *machah*.[13] One day the Lord will completely blot out our enemies—Satan, this present world system, and the flesh or sin. Yet I want you to see another beautiful use of the word *machah*.

David uses *machah* twice in one of my favorite psalms:

¹*Have mercy on me, O God,*
    according to your unfailing love;
according to your great compassion
    blot out my transgressions....

⁹*Hide your face from my sins*
    and blot out all my iniquity. (Psalm 51:1, 9 NIV)

When I put the words "blot out" in the context of my sins, my heart cries, "Oh Lord, let it be! Cleanse me completely." I have to admit that at times the justice of God is hard for me to accept and understand, but if I am truly honest, His unrelenting mercy is even harder to comprehend. In the end, I choose to trust the discernment of a God who is willing to "blot out" my sins simply based upon my faith, and who offers that opportunity to *all people*, as these verses indicate:

*The Lord is not slow to fulfill his promise as some count slowness, but is patient toward you, not wishing that any should perish, but that **all** should reach repentance.*
(2 Peter 3:9, emphasis added)

*"Say to them, As I live, declares the Lord God, **I have no pleasure in the death of the wicked**, but that the wicked turn from his way and live; turn back, turn back from your evil ways, for why will you die, O house of Israel?"*
(Ezekiel 33:11, emphasis added)

The heart of God is revealed in these Scriptures! Although completely just, God finds no pleasure in the death of the wicked but wishes that all people come to repentance.

Now, let's return to the story in 1 Samuel 15.

Compare 1 Samuel 15:3 with 1 Samuel 15:9. In what way did Saul disobey the command of God?

Extra Insight

A descendant of Agag shows up in Israelite history 500 years after this event. In the book of Esther, Haman, an Agaite, tried to annihilate the Jewish people.[14]

Saul did not obey the command of God to utterly destroy the Amalekites and keep none of the loot. He had forgotten his place. As king, he was to serve beneath the authority of almighty God. The kingship was not a position of power but of service. In that moment, Saul was no longer serving God, nor was he leading God's people.

According to 1 Samuel 15:11, what was God's response?

God rejected Saul's position as king and would choose another willing to serve to take his place. When the Lord "regrets" or "repents," it is not the same as when we do. When we repent, we change our will, submitting it once again to God's. When God "regrets" or "repents," He is not changing His will but willing a change. In other words, God is choosing to go a different direction to accomplish His divine, perfect will. God would choose a different person to carry out His will. If Saul would not obey, then God would find another who would.

Verse 11 also tells us that Samuel was angry and cried out to the Lord all night.

Extra Insight

God's regret in choosing Saul is an example of anthropomorphism, which is when God uses human language and terms to help explain Himself to human beings. While this analogy falls short, it does help us understand His heart toward Saul.[15]

Why do you think Samuel was so angry?

What kind of things do you think he cried out to God about all night?
Was he having a pity party, lacking trust and questioning God? Explain.

How excited do you think Samuel was to approach Saul the next morning? Have you ever wanted to just be done with something and yet, somehow, you kept getting dragged back into it? Perhaps that's how Samuel felt. Perhaps he had some personal regret regarding his relationship with Saul. In any case, he was surely tired after wrestling with God all night about his feelings.

What about you? Are you tired from wrestling with God over anything? Are you questioning His direction or lack of direction? Are you questioning His motives or love? If so, maybe a good place to start is to simply pray: "God, give me eyes to see and ears to hear. Lord, allow me to learn all You want me to learn."

Read 1 Samuel 15:12. As Samuel set out to bring God's message to Saul, what did Samuel discover at Carmel? What had Saul built?

After building a monument to himself, Saul continued on to Gilgal where he threw a massive victory party. He was feeling great about what he had accomplished for God. When Samuel showed up, Saul said, "Blessed be you to the Lord. I have performed the commandment of the Lord" (v. 13). He truly didn't see his disobedience or hear it for that matter, though it was totally evident to Samuel when he heard the lowing of the Amalekites' sheep (v. 14). But all Saul could hear was the roar of his ego. He literally could not see his own failure. He was in total denial.

Listen, friend, sometimes we are blind to our own sins. It's interesting how other people find them so apparent and yet we just can't see them. It is so easy to see someone else's faults and pay no mind to our own. This is why the words of Psalm 139:23-24 should often be the cry of our hearts and the words on our lips:

> ²³*Search me, O God, and know my heart!*
> *Try me and know my thoughts!*
> ²⁴*And see if there be any grievous way in me,*
> *and lead me in the way everlasting!*

Saul was celebrating something that never should have been celebrated. God did not want his offerings but his obedience. God did not desire the defeated enemy king to be paraded through the land of Israel as a trophy for Saul. This was to be an act of swift judgment—something that, according to Ezekiel 33:11, brings God no pleasure. If God finds no pleasure in it, then Saul should not either. The annihilation of a people was not something to be celebrated or boasted.

With my eyes still focused on Saul's newly erected image, my heart ponders the words of Samuel to Saul in 1 Samuel 15:17 as he began to confront Saul with what he had done: "Though you are little in your own eyes...." Could it be that the more insecure we are, the more prideful we become in order to conceal it? The smaller we feel, the bigger the images we build? The more out of control we feel, the more we strive for control?

Could it be that the more insecure we are, the more prideful we become in order to conceal it?

Read 1 Samuel 15:17-21. How did Saul respond to the accusations of Samuel?

Did you notice that the very thing Saul was using as proof of his obedience actually was the proof of his disobedience? He was literally calling Agag to the witness stand. I bet Samuel wanted to say, "Dude, Agag is not *your* witness; he is actually the star witness for the *prosecution*."

Finally, when all else had failed, Saul blamed the people. Whoa, first total denial, then rationalization: "But the people took of the spoil, sheep and oxen, the best of the things devoted to destruction, to sacrifice to the LORD your God in Gilgal" (v. 21).

Summarize Samuel's response to this rationalization found in verses 22-23.

Commentator David Guzik writes, "One could make a thousand sacrifices unto God; work a thousand hours for God's service; or give millions of dollars to His work. But all of those sacrifices mean little if there is not a surrendered heart to God, shown by simple obedience."[16]

Are you beginning to see the layers of protection that Saul was placing around himself? He seemed to be running from surrender. Friend, strip away your defense mechanisms and lay your surrendered heart before a merciful God. Don't protect. Release your grip and grow!

Prayer Prompt

Ask God to show you any areas of your life where you are choosing control over surrender.

DAY 5

Scripture Focus

1 Samuel 15:24-35;
16:1-13

Today our reading seems to begin with such hope as Saul confesses, "I have sinned." Yet quickly we question his motivation. Were these words of true surrender, or were they just another attempt at control?

Read 1 Samuel 15:24-31 and record your insights regarding Saul's repentance. What elements are there? What seems to be missing? What was Saul's greatest concern?

Saul said the words "I have sinned," but in the same breath he rationalized that he was just afraid of his people. I'm not sure I buy that, though. He didn't fear his people when he commanded them to fast through an entire battle (14:24). If my son had not eaten in a couple of days, I definitely would fear him. He got really "hangry." Can you imagine an entire army of hangry men?

It was not the king's job to fear the people but to lead them. The buck stopped at Saul. This defense was weak, and in this moment, so was Saul. One thing seemed to be missing from Saul's words: sincerity. I do not see any broken spirit over his disobedience. Instead, he continued to request Samuel's presence at the great sacrifice. I'm paraphrasing here, but it sounds like, "Samuel, I get it. I screwed up, but don't make a scene. This is not a good time for us to publicize our break-up. Let's finish this sacrifice, and we will talk later."

Samuel seemed to nearly come out of his skin with this request. I can just see his red face as he screamed his emphatic "no" and once again tried to make Saul understand what he had done and the consequences for it. As Samuel turned to storm out, Saul grabbed his robe and tore it.

I imagine the most intense scene here. If you will allow me to paint a picture, I see time slowing down as Samuel uses all his strength to reel in his emotion and glare into the eyes of Saul. With words like daggers, he states, "This is exactly what the Lord will do to your kingdom. He will give it to someone else and, let me be clear, He will not regret it!"

Seemingly unmoved, Saul once again requested Samuel's presence at the sacrifice. I really wish that I could see the body language in this scene. I would like to see the eyes of Saul as he requested or maybe even demanded Samuel's presence at the public sacrifice. Don't forget, he was the king—for now anyway. He was the king who had just led his people in battle and destroyed one of their most historic enemies. This might not have been the best time for Samuel to cross him.

Read 1 Samuel 15:32-33. What did Samuel request in return for going to the sacrifice?

What did he do with this prisoner?

Upon Samuel's return from the sacrifice, it seems that when he encountered the smug arrogance of Agag, he snapped. He hacked the enemy king to pieces. *Wow, that is some kind of rage!* I cannot help but wonder if some of that rage was misplaced. Samuel was fed up with arrogance. He may have been frustrated because his words were no longer being respected or heeded. So I wonder, could Agag have been the recipient of some of the rage Samuel felt toward Saul?

This scene reminds me of a quotation from Friedrich Nietzsche: "He who fights with monsters should be careful lest he thereby become a monster. And if thou gaze long into an abyss, the abyss will also gaze into thee."[17]

If we were watching this scene in a movie, would Samuel be considered a hero or a fallen hero? Regardless of what was or was not happening within Samuel, here's an important point for each of us: we'd better be careful not to demonize anyone. We can be so intent on destroying the "monster" that we become one. We tend to hack away at the things we hate most within ourselves.

Read 1 Samuel 15:34-35. How would you describe the tone at the end of this chapter?

This was obviously the end of any relationship between Samuel and Saul. Samuel did not see Saul again until the day of his death. Scripture says in verse 35, "But Samuel grieved over Saul. And the LORD regretted that he had made Saul king over Israel." These words almost seem like a loop playing in the heart of Samuel (1 Samuel 15:11). But I do not believe that Samuel's grief over Saul was all about Saul. I believe Samuel had deep personal regrets regarding how he had handled things with Saul—regrets that forged ruts in Samuel's thinking. It seems that any time a relationship ends, there are regrets on both sides, no matter the circumstances.

We all have scars, don't we? We all have deep wounds and regrets. These traumas have a way of habitually working their way into our thoughts. Out of the blue, a painful memory will arise, and the emotion that accompanies it seems so raw and fresh. This is the battle for the mind, and we need the Lord to fight for us and bring His victory in our lives.

Read Psalm 51:7-8 in the margin. Which part of this verse speaks to you and why? In what ways do you need the Lord's restoration in your life?

Soak me in your laundry and I'll come out clean, scrub me and I'll have a snow-white life. Tune me in to foot-tapping songs, set these once-broken bones to dancing.
(Psalm 51:7-8 MSG)

It's common to grieve upon the death of someone, right? Yet Saul is still alive. I can't help but wonder everything Samuel is grieving over. The death of a reign? The death of a dream? The death of his relationship with Saul? What kind of things might have died within Samuel himself during this reign of Saul?

I can relate to this kind of grief. In many ways divorce is similar. I grieve over the death of the marriage while the man I was married to is still alive. I grieve over a broken covenant. I grieve over a broken family. I grieve over lost potential. I grieve over my own mistakes. I grieve over what it cost me.

It takes time to grieve, but we cannot let grief swallow us up. It is okay not to be okay, but we cannot stay in that place too long. After all that Samuel had been through with Saul, God told Samuel, "Okay, it is time to move forward."

Read 1 Samuel 16:1-13. What do you think the words "I have provided for myself a king" (vs. 1) mean?

It takes time to grieve, but we cannot let grief swallow us up.

Could God be suggesting that with Saul, God gave the people of Israel the type of king *they* wanted, but with David, God would be choosing the type of king H*e* wanted? The difference between the two would not seem evident at times based on outward behavior, but it would be revealed in the sincerity of David's heart.

Samuel no longer seemed to be the same confident prophet he once was. He was afraid (v. 2). According to verses 4-5, he wasn't the only one who was afraid. The word of tension between Samuel and Saul had made its way throughout the land. Samuel's fear caused him anxiety, and this anxiety drove his need for control and certainty. Instead of trusting God for each step, he wanted a blueprint laid out. God graciously gave the old prophet added information. Remember, even great men and women of God can have moments of fear. Just read the stories of Elijah or Esther!

What did God tell Samuel to do once he arrived at the home of Jesse (v. 3)?

Read 1 Samuel 16:6-13. What stands out to you about the scene and how David was anointed? Write about or draw the scene as it unfolded. Don't worry about being a great artist!

When Samuel saw Eliab, Jesse's oldest son, he thought, *Oh yeah, this guy looks like a king.* Funny, because that's what everyone thought about Saul, too. The old prophet was being deceived by the very thing we all are so often deceived by—outer appearance. The people had been through that circus already. This time God would pick someone sincere in heart.

After going through the lineup, God still had not chosen any of the sons of Jesse. Samuel asked Jesse, "Are all your sons here?" And Jesse responded, "There remains yet the youngest, but behold, he is keeping the sheep" (v. 11).

This whole scene cracks me up. Let's compare the stories of Saul and David. Saul was the prized son of his father. He was what every father would want in a son. He was valued and protected. Remember when he went out in search of the donkeys and his father sent a servant along with him, probably both for guidance and protection. After three days with no word, the father was worried when Saul had not returned.

In Jesse, we have a father who, when asked to line up his sons for some great honor, didn't even consider his youngest. The fact that David was a shepherd tells us that not only did the family not have servants, but David *was* the servant. Shepherding was a servant's job, unless you didn't have any servants. Then it became the job of the lowest man on the totem pole, the youngest son. David cared for multitudes of sheep all alone in the fields, while Saul needed a chaperone to find three lost donkeys. (I still wonder who lost those donkeys in the first place!)

I find it interesting that the more difficult background produced the man with the sincere heart. It seems, once again, that hardship is our greatest teacher and solitude our greatest classroom.

Read 1 Samuel 16:12-13 again. How is young David described in these verses?

Basically, David was a young boy with a fair complexion and beautiful light eyes. When you saw him, you would think, *What a beautiful boy.* You wouldn't think, *Man he looks like a king.* But isn't that the point the Lord was making?

Read Zechariah 4:6 in the margin. How would you explain this verse in your own words?

Here's the context for this verse. God had given Zechariah a vision to encourage Zerubbabel, who had been commissioned to rebuild the temple after the Babylonian exile, to faithfully finish the work. Zerubbabel had become discouraged, and God was reminding Him that the work would not be accomplished by human might or resources but by His! God would provide as effortlessly as if two olive trees were pouring oil directly into the golden lamp stand (Zecharaiah 4:1-5).

The connection to our story in 1 Samuel 16 is evident. The success of the kingship would not be about any man's ability but about God's ability. A branch will only produce life-giving fruit when it abides in the vine (John 15:4). I don't know about you, but I would like to spend more time abiding and producing and less time controlling and conjuring!

Extra Insight

"Contemporary North American society would have us all be Saul's instead of David's....Yes, we are fearfully and wonderfully made in God's image, but we do the Bible a great disservice when we try to show how these truths lead to self-esteem boosting and puffing up our egos....David did not achieve greatness because he nurtured narcissism."[18]

"This is the word of the LORD to Zerubbabel: Not by might, nor by power, but by my Spirit, says the LORD of hosts."
(Zechariah 4:6)

Prayer Prompt

Spend some time worshiping today. Turn on your favorite meditation music and just abide in the goodness of God. With each inhale and exhale, repeat Zechariah 4:6 (in the margin). Allow this verse to flow through you as a reminder that God is in control. He holds all things together. It's not up to you!

His words have the power to bring _____.

His words have the power to set the _____ _____.

His words have the power to _____.

His words have the power to _____ _____.

Don't let your past _____ you. Let it _____ you.

Words are powerful, and they can have a _____ _____.

When it comes to who you are, God's _____ is what counts.

Scriptures: Genesis 1, John 1, Colossians 2:9, John 14:7, John 12:49, Mark 4:35-41, Mark 5, 1 Corinthians 14:3, 1 Samuel 12, Psalm 139:23-24, Proverbs 25:11, Proverbs 18:21, Matthew 12:34

Week 4

Crud, I'm Completely Out of Control

Facing Our Fear When the Wheels Come Off

1 Samuel 16–21

DAY 1

We are at the half-way point of our study, and we have just witnessed the anointing of young David as the next king, when "the Spirit of the Lᴏʀᴅ rushed upon David from that day forward" (1 Samuel 16:13). We begin our lesson today with the next verse, and it's a doozy!

Scripture Focus

1 Samuel 16:14-23

Write 1 Samuel 16:14 below.

We need to spend some time breaking this one down. We have to be careful not to read this verse through our New Testament lenses. The continual indwelling of the Holy Spirit did not take place until after the resurrection. In the Old Testament, the Spirit of God would temporarily indwell or "come upon" different individuals to empower them to fulfill God's purposes. The Spirit of God has now come upon David, anointing him as king, and so the Spirit has departed from Saul.

God had empowered Saul to see and do things he normally would not be able to do. He had given Saul a calling and a purpose, which comes with responsibility. If Saul were unwilling to obey the commands of God, then God would choose another.

We can track with that. But what do we make of the second part of the verse: "A harmful spirit from the Lᴏʀᴅ tormented him"? The word *torment* here is *ba'ath*, which means "to fall upon, startle, terrify."[1] This sounds like a possible anxiety attack to me! That heightened fight or flight instinct was not Saul's permanent state; rather, these were periodic episodes that surely scared not only Saul, but also all who watched.

I have had seasons of extreme anxiety, and I am telling you I would not wish it on my worst enemy. It is a fear that swallows up all logic. No matter how much I prayed, read my Bible, or acknowledged the illogical fears I was experiencing, I could not convince my body not to panic.

Yet, as we read this verse, the part that is most alarming is the phrase "from the Lord." Why would God send Saul into a panic? Without taking up too much space, allow me to address this. The Jewish people believed that God was sovereign over all things. Therefore, they credited all events to Him, good and bad, in the sense that nothing happens without God's knowledge and allowance.

For example, in the story of Job, Satan was the agent of Job's troubles. Yet the devil had to ask for God's permission. Mark 5 shows another example of the sovereignty of God when the demoniac bows down at the authority of Jesus. Not only is God sovereign over the supernatural, but He is sovereign over the natural as well. When the Creator speaks, creation must obey. God has the power to heal and raise the dead. Therefore, as divine Creator, He is sovereign over all aspects of our world.

Yet does God's sovereignty make Him the agent of delivery for bad events? At times, we give God credit for doing something that was actually the result of free will, earthly processes, or the enemy. For example, in Genesis 30, did God actually show His *approval* of Rachel's decision to give her servant Bilhah to Jacob by granting her a son? Was God actually a part of that cat fight? In I Samuel 2:6, Hannah proclaims, "The Lord kills and brings to life." Does God actually kill? These are challenging but important questions.

Summarize each of the following Scriptures:

James 1:13

1 John 1:5

1 Corinthians 14:33

If God won't tempt someone to do evil, would He send an evil spirit to torment a person? Can the author of peace send confusion? Share your thoughts about how we might reconcile these New Testament Scriptures with the Old Testament examples mentioned on the previous page.

These are the kinds of practical questions we struggle with every day. A young man was dating a girl he truly believed was the one. He loved her, yet in time they broke up. He struggled and continued to ask God to bring them back together, because he was convinced she was the one. A few months later they began talking once more. He was sure that this was from God. God had answered his prayers! When once again things did not work out, he was confused and angry with God. Why would God bring them back together just for this to happen? Good question.

The better question is, *Did God bring them back together*? Did God "allow" or did He "bring"? When asked that question, the young man responded, "Either way, God is mean! I have asked God to give me the desire of my heart and, if He chooses not to, to please remove the desire from me." That sounds really good, doesn't it? But it is bad theology!

The young man essentially was asking God to either give him what he wanted or take away his pain immediately. That is not realistic. He hadn't considered that God *allowed* them to get back together to show them both that the relationship was not right for either of them. God is not in the business of magically removing our pain, but He will allow pain to be our teacher.

The fact is, in His sovereignty, God did *allow* torment to reign in Saul, whether demonic or mental anguish. But "to allow" and "to be the agent of delivery" are two very different things. In 1 Samuel 16:14, the author is not interested in secondary causation, but due to his belief that God is Lord of all, gives full credit to God for this evil spirit, even though He didn't *cause* it.

> **God is not in the business of magically removing our pain, but He will allow pain to be our teacher.**

Read Proverbs 1:23-33. In light of this proverb, what was Saul's responsibility for his own situation?

Commentaries vary in their descriptions of this spirit that plagued Saul. Some view it as demonic[2] while others interpret it as an injurious, bad, or dark mood.[3] Personally, I think that when the Spirit of the Lord departed from Saul, he was left to his own devices. God's anointing was gone—and God's empowerment and covering along with it. Saul seems to have felt this to his core.

All the things Saul was prone to demonstrate only appear to have intensified: fear, paranoia, narcissism, and mood swings. The years of war, the words of Samuel, and his own fear of failure apparently took their toll. He had built a great dam of self-protection, and now this dam was beginning to crack. My heart longs to cry out to Saul, "Repent, the role of king has passed, but a relationship with God can still be found!"

What areas of your life are you trying hard to conceal or control? How long do you think your dam will hold?

Read 1 Samuel 16:15-23.

What solution did Saul's servants suggest for his mental anguish?

Who is named in verse 18, and how is he described?

As we read these verses, we discover that there are some chronological issues here. For example, in 1 Samuel 16:18, we see that Saul's servant gave David some kudos that seem premature. How could this young shepherd boy be all of these things when he hadn't even fought Goliath yet? Another example is 1 Samuel 16:21. David would not become Saul's armor-bearer until after the slaying of the giant. What are we to make of this?

Think about telling a story and then going back later and filling in the gaps with better, stronger details. Depending on the point of the story, those added details are likely necessary to give someone a fuller picture. Though we can't be sure, I suspect that might have happened here with the writer of 1 Samuel.

Considering the fact that Jesse's son had already been anointed the future king, what do you think might have been running through Jesse's mind when Saul summoned his son? Had word of David's anointing gotten out? Could this concern have motivated Jesse to pile more gifts on that ole donkey? We don't have solid answers to these questions, but in the end, we get the information we truly need: young David came to the palace to play music for the king.

Do you see the beauty in this? God sent the future king to soothe the reigning one. David was not there to threaten but to soothe. The Hebrew word for *soothe* is *ravach*, and it means to be wide or spacious, to breathe easily, or to be relieved.[4] In other words, when the walls were caving in on Saul, David brought the open space and peace of the pasture. David's music allowed Saul to breathe!

Music is an amazing thing, isn't it?

Read Job 38:4-7 and Revelation 5:8-10. What role does music play in each passage? What seems to be its purpose?

Do you see it? There was singing when the earth was formed, and there will be singing after the earth is gone. The harmony of the Trinity rings throughout the pages of Scripture. No wonder there should be a song in our hearts—music is a gift from God! A gift we enjoy because we were made in His image.

Did you know that researchers have discovered how music can calm anxiety?[5] They saw that brain waves begin to sync up with the rhythm of the music,[6] creating mental states that coincide with the type of music played. With this knowledge, musicologists have created entire playlists designed to decrease your heart rate.

I can imagine the racing heartbeat of Saul beginning to slow as he listened to the sounds coming from the lyre of David (1 Samuel 16:23). A young boy bringing the open spaces of a shepherd to a tortured king.

Several years ago, a neighbor knocked on our door at an unusually late hour. His wife was having a psychotic break, and he needed our help while he called the doctor. We entered their home to find her screaming uncontrollably. To be honest, I would have described this as "a tormenting spirit." My

Extra Insight

A lyre (or *kinnor* in ancient Hebrew) was a handheld instrument that resembled a small harp. In Saul's time, the *kinnor* had between 3 to 12 gut strings. It was played with a plectrum (an ancient pick) when accompanying singing or dancing, but was usually plucked with the fingers when played alone.[7]

husband and I rushed over to her. The only thing I could think to do at the time was to sing. I started to sing every worship song I could possibly think of. When I did, the most amazing thing happened. She stopped. As long as I was singing, she was still. The minute I stopped, the torment would once again have its grip. The power of worship was evident to me that day!

In the end, I believe the unrepentant sin of Saul did exactly what Psalm 32:3-4 tells us it will do:

> ³When I kept it all inside,
>   my bones turned to powder,
>   my words became daylong groans.
>
> ⁴The pressure never let up;
>   all the juices of my life dried up. (MSG)

And yet in the midst of Saul's pain, God brought David to offer relief. Only God could bring the future king into the palace both to prepare David and to soothe Saul. Only the pride of Saul could turn this gift into his enemy.

Finish today's study by listening to some music. Take some deep breaths as you listen, and allow God to minister to your soul.

Prayer Prompt

Pour out to the Prince of Peace any fears that you might have today, asking Him to give you the clarity and faith to face any current bullies you may be up against. Above all, spend time reminding yourself whom you serve. There is nothing impossible with God—and don't forget, He happens to delight in you!

DAY 2

Scripture Focus

1 Samuel 17:1-30

As we noted in our lesson yesterday, 1 Samuel 16 ends with some confusing chronological issues. Whether or not David was summoned to play music for King Saul before or after the famous showdown we're going to explore today, chapter 17 opens with David back in the fields tending sheep as the Philistines are gathering their armies to fight Israel.

Read 1 Samuel 17:1-11.

Describe the scene we find in verses 1-3.

Describe Goliath and his armor (vv. 4-7).

What is Goliath's proposition?

The Philistines were one of the first civilizations to enter the Iron Age. They used this iron to forge weapons and armor. This combination of weaponry and military allowed them to hold the three major cities along the Via Maris, the great trade route that ran along the Mediterranean Sea.[8] One of the few roads that connected these coastal cities with the territories of Jerusalem and Bethlehem ran right through the valley of Elah. This made it important ground for battle. The Israelites had to hold their position in order to protect the rest of Judah from the Philistines.[9]

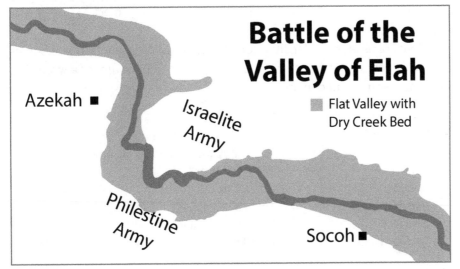

The two armies gathered on opposite mountains with the valley between. This valley is not expansive, so each army had a good view of the other's encampment. Therefore, when Goliath, the champion for the Philistines, challenged the Israelites, they easily could have heard and seen him. It would have been quite the scene.

According to Strong's Concordance, the Hebrew word for *champion* means "the man between the two" and describes where Goliath stood—between the Philistine and Israelite camps.[10] Goliath essentially came walking out crying, "mano a mano," literally a challenge to hand-to-hand combat.[11] Why waste good men on the battlefield when they can become slaves for the victor?

This giant was somewhere between nine and ten feet tall and carried around approximately two hundred pounds of armor. This was one big giant, and he could talk some smack!

Look again at verse 11. How did the Israelites react to Goliath?

Isn't this what bullies do? Their whole purpose is to strike fear in the hearts of their prey. Think about it. If a bully can create fear, he has already created an advantage for himself and possibly won the battle. On one hand, the opponent may be so scared he chooses not to engage. On the other, if he does engage, he is doing so with great apprehension.

My son was the starting safety on the Stanford football team. If he could get in an opponent's head before the play, he was already a step ahead. The opponent would either avoid the hit altogether or play with fear. If you play afraid, you will not focus on catching the pass. Talking smack is just part of the game.

Plenty of us face similar situations today. We all face giants, those bullies who strike fear in our hearts. Maybe it's a person, a pressure, or a worry, but we all face some kind of giant.

Addiction:	"You will never be free!"
Self-worth:	"You will never be enough!"
Anger:	"Everybody will always let me down!"
Rejection:	"This will never last!"
Comfort:	"Don't rock the boat!"
Bad marriage:	"There is no hope!"
Finances:	"It is never enough!"
Wayward child:	"It's all my fault!"

Does the voice of one of these giants ring in your ears? If so, what does it say to you?

Bullies cause so much hurt because their words often contain a small bit of truth in them. My daughter experienced this in grade school. One of the boys at her school continually made fun of her for being overweight. Every time she would sit down on the bench, he would bounce up as if the force of her body knocked him off. He would say things like, "Oh, watch out for Hillary sitting down." He not only embarrassed her but also badly hurt her feelings. When she told us about it, her father found the perfect opportunity to talk to the young boy. He handled it beautifully, getting the point across to this young man that Hillary belonged to him and whoever messed with her would be messing with him! The young boy got the message and stopped the teasing.

The teasing hurt Hillary so much because at the time, she was heavier than many of her classmates, and this bothered her tremendously. This bully knew exactly how to stick his finger in her wounds.

> Take time to reflect further on the giant you identified on the previous page. Look into the "accountability mirror" and tell yourself the truth. Beat the giant to the punch! Do you know when you began to struggle with this fear? Were there any experiences or traumas in your past that served as triggers? What have you done to fight the battle, and how has this worked for you?

Whatever our particular struggle might be, we do not face our battles alone. We too have a heavenly Father who says, "That girl belongs to me. I made her in my image, and not only is she good, she is *very* good. I knit her together in her mother's womb where I knew her intimately. I know everything about her, and trust me, she is worth dying for. When you mess with her, you mess with me!"

Read 1 Samuel 17:12-16.

Which sons of Jesse had gone with Saul to battle? Write their names below.

How long did the giant torment Israel morning and evening?

Tucked within this famous story is an interesting verse about the giant's tactics in taunting the people of Israel.

Read 1 Samuel 1:16. When did the giant do this, and for how long?

Read Genesis 7:12, Joshua 5:6, and Matthew 4:1-2. What do these verses have in common?

The number forty, whether days or years, seems to be used in Scripture as a period of testing and/or judgment. So, for forty days this giant tested the faith of Israel. Did you also notice that he came out both in the morning and in the evening? I don't know about you, but it seems that my giants tend to scream the loudest in the morning when I open my eyes, and in the evening when I lay my head down on the pillow. If you are still struggling to pinpoint your giants, consider what you worry about when you lay your head down at night.

Read 1 Samuel 17:17-27. What did Jesse ask David to do?

What was David's response after seeing and hearing Goliath?

Having been out in the fields tending his father's sheep, David set out to join his brothers on the battlefield. Loaded up with gifts and responsibility, he was sent off by his father with the instructions to send back word regarding the well-being of his brothers. After securing the care of his sheep, David left early in the morning and made it to the battlefield just in time to drop his baggage and join the army at the frontlines. And behold, here came Goliath!

David could not believe his eyes or ears. At the sound of the giant's voice, the army of Israel began to crumble. Despite the passionate speeches by the commanders reminding the men what would be done for the man who defeated Goliath, the army retreated in fear. In the middle of this chaos, young David tried to get clarification on what he'd just heard. "Wait. What is the king going to do for the man who kills Goliath?" And then he made a powerful statement: "Who is this uncircumcised Philistine that he should defy the armies of the living God?" (NIV).

I can't help but think of another story that involves giants. Let's go there for a minute.

Read Numbers 13:25-33. When the ten unfaithful spies saw the giants in the promised land, what did they say they felt like (v. 33)?

Do you really think *all* the people in the land were of great height? Even if they were, this is all about perception. Fear causes us to lose perspective. It is the great exaggerator! When the spies compared themselves with the giants, they felt like grasshoppers. Yet if they had compared the giants to God, guess who would have looked like grasshoppers?

David looked at this uncircumcised Philistine and compared him to God. Who was this *man* to defy the living *God*!

Think about what you are afraid of right now. Have you allowed fear to magnify your situation, convincing you that victory is impossible? Are you attempting to fight your giant in your own strength or in God's strength?

> **Fear causes us to lose perspective. It is the great exaggerator!**

The key to facing any battle is to know your "why." If your "why" is big enough, you will engage. And trust me, your "why" better be big, because some battles don't take just one stone. Some battles last a long time, and in the end, you will have the scars to prove it. But if your "why" is big enough, the scars will be worth it.

Read 1 Samuel 17:28-30. Who seemed to have a problem with David's "why"?

Eliab, David's oldest brother, immediately shot David down. He began by trying to make David feel insignificant. "Why have you come down? And with whom have you left those few sheep in the wilderness?" (v. 28). Wow, who peed in his cereal? Why was he making David feel insignificant? Could it be because Eliab felt that way? I suggest that he remembered the oil dripping off of his baby brother's head. Now David had shown up here unshaken by this giant.

Second, Eliab questioned David's motives. "I know your pride and the insolence of your heart" (v. 28 NKJV). Did he really know David's heart? It seems to me that David's heart was pretty pure at the moment. If I had been David and my older brother had insulted me and asked why I was there, I would have said, "Oh, really? Why are *you* here? Obviously, it's not to fight!" Yep, I would have gotten punched, I'm sure! When we feel injured, threatened, or judged, we often want to throw the first punch by attacking the other person's motives, projecting our hurt onto the other person. It is one of the greatest defense mechanisms we have.

David heard the criticism of his brother and chose not to engage. Instead, he focused on the bigger issue. We can learn a lot from David. He chose not to fight his brother, but instead chose to fight the enemy.

Based on his words below, it seems that Theodore Roosevelt understood what it's like to get a little criticism.

> It is not the critic who counts; not the man who points out how the strong man stumbles, or where the doer of deeds could have done them better. The credit belongs to the man who is actually in the arena, whose face is marred by dust and sweat and blood; who strives valiantly; who errs and comes short again and again, because there is no effort without error and shortcoming; but who does actually strive to do the deeds; who knows great enthusiasms, the great devotions; who spends himself in a worthy cause; who at the best knows in the end the triumph of high achievement, and who at the worst, if he fails, at least fails while daring greatly, so that his place shall never be with those cold and timid souls who neither know victory nor defeat.[12]

Don't let criticism keep you from moving forward. If your "why" is big enough, a little criticism from the naysayers will not stop you.

Prayer Prompt

Spend some time with your Father today and evaluate the battles you are currently facing. Are they your battles to fight? If so, what is your "why"? If for some reason the naysayers have gotten you off track, ask God to give you renewed focus and resolve.

DAY 3

Yesterday we ended our lesson with David speaking with his brother Eliab about the big "why" for fighting the giant. David's bold words reached the ears of King Saul, and that is where we pick up today.

Scripture Focus

1 Samuel 17:31–18:1-4

Read 1 Samuel 17:31-37, and summarize the exchange between Saul and David in your own words.

Word had gotten back to Saul that there was one who was willing to fight the giant. When David walked into the room and said, "Everything is alright, guys. I've got this. It's all under control," I wish I could have seen the expressions in the room. Saul looked at David and said, "Young man, this giant has been fighting longer than you have been alive!" (my paraphrase).

Although this was true, there was something powerful about this young man's courage and his willingness to put his life on the line to fight. Some would argue that this was all David had to put on the line because, whether man or woman, a young person typically does not have much to lose. But what happens to us when we accumulate things, build a reputation, and become providers for those we love? Do we continue to show courage when the stakes get high? David's courage was infectious, and this was just the virus that Israel needed to catch right then!

When Saul questioned David's ability and experience, David reached down into his "cookie jar" for a past victory. I was first introduced to the "cookie jar" method by a present-day David, David Goggins, who has been deemed the "toughest man alive."[13] It is a good thing he is the toughest, because he would agree that he has not always been the smartest. Yet nothing in his life has been wasted, and to remind himself of this, he has created something he calls the "cookie jar method":

> The cookie jar is a place in my mind where I put all things bad and good that shaped me. Some people try to forget the bad in their life. I use my bad for strength when needed, great lessons learned. In that cookie jar, I pull out whatever I need for the task at hand.[14]

David Goggins puts not only his defeats in the cookie jar, but also his many victories. When facing an overwhelming challenge, he is able to take out a cookie, take a bite, and gain whatever motivation he needs to meet the challenge head-on.

When our young David opened his cookie jar, he could recall victories over a lion and a bear. If he could defeat those fierce beasts, then he felt he could defeat the giant, too.

As human beings, we have a propensity to remember the bad events of our lives more than the positive. We remember our defeats much more than our victories. Studies using magnetic resonance imaging (MRI) have shown that negative events stimulate activity in the emotion-processing regions of the brain, such as the orbital frontal cortex and the amygdala. The more these emotional regions are activated, the more likely we are to remember the details of the event. In other words, we typically dissect every detail of a negative event—primarily to prevent it from happening again.[15] We have to be vigilant about counteracting this tendency by remembering our victories.

Throughout the Scriptures, God instructs His people to set up memorials reminding them of their victories. Clearly, David knew the value of remembering his victories, and King Saul gave David his blessing to go after Goliath.

Now read 1 Samuel 17:38-39. What did Saul place on David?

I will forever have questions about this scene. Why in the world would Saul think his armor would fit David? Perhaps Saul was trying to make a point. Maybe he was attempting to slow David down because the word had gotten out that David was the next anointed king. Or *if* David possibly had been Saul's musician before the fight with Goliath, which has been debated,[16] could it be that Saul was legitimately trying to protect his musician? There is no way for us to know, but what we do know is that Saul's armor did not fit. The armor was not the important point here. Saul had the armor, yet he didn't have the heart.

Has there been a time in your life when you had the armor but not the heart? What good was the armor to you in that situation?

What does David say in verse 39? Write his words below.

David could not go into battle with someone else's armor. It wasn't his "cookie jar"!

Friend, there is only one you. No one else has the beautiful combination of gifts and talents that you do. No one else has the upbringing you do—all the events that molded you into who you are. We all face battles and we all must reach into our own cookie jar for strength. There is not a battle that God has called you to face that He has not also equipped you to win.

Take some time to write down your victories and defeats. What are some of the events that have molded you into who you are? How did they make you feel? What did you learn or how did you grow? Put all of these things in your cookie jar.

No one else has the beautiful combination of gifts and talents that you do.

COOKIE JAR

Event	How I felt	What I learned / How I grew
Victories		
Defeats		

Finish reading the story of David and Goliath in 1 Samuel 17:40-58, and list below all of the contrasts in this battle. For example, the difference in voices, weapons, size, and demeanor.

David   Goliath

Now faith is the assurance of things hoped for, the conviction of things not seen.

(Hebrews 11:1)

I remember the time my son was asked to pray before a school basketball game. When he began, his middle school adolescent voice cracked when he said the words, "Dear Lord." He just about died! Can you imagine the difference between the sound of Goliath's voice and David's voice?

Bottom line: This was not a fair fight. Goliath knew this, and it actually made him mad. The mere sight of David was an insult to him! Be careful, Goliath, "Pride goeth...before a fall" (Proverbs 16:18 KJV). How many sports teams have lost because they underestimated the sight of their opponent?

Oh, but isn't that the point? According to everything one could see, this battle would be over before it even began. Yet something could not be seen: "I come to you in the name of the Lord of hosts" (1 Samuel 17:45). The beauty of this story is in everything unseen. This was not a battle of brawn but of heart, of faith (Hebrews 11:1). The winning weapon was actually not a sling and a stone but faith—the conviction of the unseen!

Saul took notice of David's courage and faith, and apparently Saul's son Jonathan did as well. The scene continues in the first verses of chapter 18, where we've come to the end of a battle and the start of a significant friendship.

Write 1 Samuel 18:1 below.

What a beautiful verse! What was it about David that drew Jonathan in? It seems as though these two young men had an instant connection. The Scripture says that "the soul of Jonathan was knit to the soul of David." Could this be a biblical reference to the modern-day concept of a "soul mate"? I would have loved to hear all that David said to Saul after his victory over Goliath, but whatever he said, apparently it ignited the heart of Jonathan. He seemed to realize right then that he and David were cut from the same cloth.

Reflect on all we've studied thus far, and list below ways that David and Jonathan were alike and different. (Refer to Week 3 if you like, especially Day 3 and Day 5.)

Alike   Different

They were both courageous, confident, and faithful. Both seemed to be natural leaders and were loved by the people, but they came from very different backgrounds. Jonathan grew up in a palace, but David worked in a pasture. One was the crowned prince while the other his anointed competition.

Who had more to lose from David's presence, Saul or Jonathan? Why?

Read 1 Samuel 18:2-4. Why do you think Saul refused to let David go back home at this point? (Also refer to 1 Samuel 14:52.)

Extra Insight

Charles Swindoll calls David an "intern incognito." What a perfect place for a future king to learn the ropes.[17]

Good or bad, Saul recognized he needed to keep David close. If loyal, this giant killer could be quite the asset to the armies of Saul, but if not loyal,

David had the potential to be one of the greatest threats to his kingdom. Remember our discussion on Week 3, Day 3 about Saul "keeping his friends close and his enemies closer"? Whichever David would prove to be, Saul knew he needed to keep a watchful eye on him. Not too hard to do when your son is his best friend.

David's courage and faith had won him the attention of both Saul and Jonathan. His previous battles and victories had prepared him for the faceoff with Goliath, and he was able to reach into his cookie jar when the chips were not in his favor. Like David, we too can recall the times and ways God has been with us in the past in order to find the strength for our present challenges.

Prayer Prompt

Take your "cookie jar" with you into your time with God, and talk with Him about the victories and defeats you recalled today (page 117). Share not only how you felt but also what you learned through each experience, listening for whatever God has to say to you in response. Bring any lingering questions or unresolved issues out into the open (God knows them anyway), asking God for insight, understanding, comfort, or peace.

DAY 4

Scripture Focus

1 Samuel 18:5-15

Yesterday we saw the spark of a new friendship between David and Jonathan, but today we will see that spark ignite into one of the deepest relationships evidenced in Scripture. Although their connection seemed instant, I believe there must have been time between verses 2 and 3 of 1 Samuel 18 to allow their connection to grow into a lifelong covenant.

A covenant is different from a contract. Let me explain the difference using the words of Rabbi Jonathan Sacks: "In a contract, two or more people come together, each pursuing their self-interest, to make a mutually advantageous exchange. In a covenant, two or more people, each respecting the dignity and integrity of the other, come together in a bond of loyalty and trust to do together what neither can achieve alone. It isn't an exchange; it's a moral commitment."[18]

The Hebrew word for covenant is *berith*. It can signify a treaty between nations, a stipulation between a monarch and his subject, or as in this case, an alliance of friendship.[19] Most often, covenants were formed including signs, sacrifices, and oaths. One great example of this is Genesis 15.

Read Genesis 15 and see if you can identify the three parts of a covenant. Write them below:

Signs/Symbols: _____

Sacrifice: _____

Oath: _____

In Genesis 15, Abram asked God for assurance regarding God's earlier promise to make him into a great nation and give his descendants the land of Israel. God responded by making a covenant. He commanded Abram to prepare sacrifices by splitting the animals in half and placing their halves opposite from each other, creating a blood path down the center. God, represented by the smoking fire pot and flaming torch, came down and passed between the halves. With this action, God was saying, "May I be like these sacrifices if I do not keep my covenant."[20] Notice that God was taking on the total responsibility for this covenant, making the covenant with Abram an unconditional covenant. Finally, God spoke an oath to Abram, once again promising that Abram's descendants would inherit the land of Israel.

Now, let's apply what we have learned to the covenant between Jonathan and David. I have assisted you with references, considering the elements in this covenant are not as neatly packed into one chapter.

Look up each Scripture and describe the elements of the covenant as noted below:

1 Samuel 18:1-4   Symbols/Signs:

_____

1 Samuel 20:30-31   Sacrifice:

_____

1 Samuel 20:12-13   Pledge/Oath:

_____

I believe this is the most beautiful and vulnerable picture of true friendship in Scripture. Jonathan removed his robe, tunic, and weapons, which *symbolized* his position as the crown prince of Israel, and gave them to David. The one who had the royal right to the throne *sacrificed* himself and his position for his friend. Then he *pledged* his allegiance to David, putting his own life on the line for his friend. And the motivation for it all? Love!

"Greater love has no one than this, that someone lay down his life for his friends."

(John 15:13)

In this is love, not that we have loved God but that he loved us and sent his Son to be the propitiation for our sins.

(1 John 4:10)

According to John 15:13 in the margin, what is the greatest expression of love?

Read Deuteronomy 7:6-9. What was the motivation behind the covenant with Abraham?

Now read 1 John 4:10 in the margin. What was God's motivation in sending Jesus?

Jesus demonstrated His love for us by offering Himself as a sacrifice. The One who had the right to rule removed His royal robes and became a man. He became vulnerable and defenseless before us unto death, and with His blood He proclaimed that "everyone who calls on the name of the Lord will be saved" (Romans 10:13).

Similarly, Jonathan removed his royal robes sacrificially. In fact, by giving his robe, tunic, and armor to David, Jonathan was proclaiming, "You will be the next king of Israel. God's hand is on you, so these rightly belong to you." Jonathan was willing to set aside his own ambition to submit to the will of God. All of which was motivated by love—love for God and love for David. Jonathan loved David more than he loved the crown.

Isn't this what friendship is all about? Shouldn't we eventually come to a place where we can take off our outer image and status with our friends for the sake of the friendship? In this age of social media, we are more concerned with making an impression than making true friends. We are more comfortable controlling a narrative than becoming vulnerable and defenseless with friends. There is such truth in these words by Scott Slayton: "You have an important choice to make—you can impress people or you can have genuine friends. When we develop real friendships, our friends will know we are not that impressive. They will see the rough edges and the ugliest things about us, but we will be known and we will be loved. That is the beauty of true friendship—it sees the ugly and it stays."[21]

True friends can rejoice in others' successes. Amy Cummins writes, "Our hesitation to celebrate the accomplishments of those around us stems from fear and self-criticism. Haven't we all, at some point or another, felt as though

"You have an important choice to make—you can impress people or you can have genuine friends."

someone else's achievements would somehow limit our own, or that their success would somehow make us a failure?"[22] Wow, after reading this quotation, Jonathan's friendship with David shines all the brighter. Yet his father, Saul, is quite a different story.

Read 1 Samuel 18:5-16.

Circle the ones named in verse 5 who viewed David's success as "good":

Saul   the people   Saul's servants   David

Whose opinion seems to be omitted?

Extra Insight

Envy is defined as "a painful and resentful awareness of an advantage enjoyed by another person joined with a desire to possess the same advantage."[23]

Have you ever been around someone who seems to turn everything they touch into gold, a friend who just seems to do everything well? In that situation, it's hard not to allow envy to creep in.

What could Saul have been envious of? Actually, what was there *not* to be envious of? David was young, courageous, handsome, successful, faithful, and growing in popularity. I can just imagine Saul looking at David and "remembering when" he also used to be young, handsome, and courageous. Remember the zeal he showed against the Ammonites when he cut the cattle into pieces and formed an army of 300,000 men (Week 2, Day 4; 1 Samuel 11:7-8). He was a strong king that day for sure! I imagine he could still hear the cries of the nation as they shouted, "Long live the king!" Yet, now in his old age, the shouts of praise likely seemed distant while the hauntings of his failures seemed near. I believe Saul saw in David something he once had, and the cancer of envy began to grow.

Is there anyone in your life right now who seems to "have it all"? That person who, no matter how hard you look, doesn't seem to show a flaw? We all can relate to the underlying problem of envy: comparison!

Motivational speaker Ed Mylett says, "Comparison and happiness cannot coexist."[24] He challenges people to look into the areas of their lives where they feel unhappy, suggesting that the root cause of this unhappiness is comparison—not only comparison with other people and what they have or do, but also comparison with previous versions of themselves. Mylett writes, "If you want to have an unhappy relationship, let me tell you how to have it…Compare it to your previous relationship! If you want to be unhappy with your fitness, compare your current body at 45 to your body when you were fit at 18!"[25]

I think Saul was doing both—comparing himself to David as well as comparing himself to his former glory. And all of this comparison fed his ever-growing virus of envy.

Take some time to evaluate the areas of your life where you feel "unhappy." Can you find any comparisons lurking around beneath those areas?

Areas of unhappiness   **Comparisons**

Saul may have been secretly envious of David, but verses 6-7 will take it to a different level.

If there is a heading above 1 Samuel 18:6 in your Bible, what is it? (See English Standard Version, Common English Bible, Good News Translation.)

The ESV heading says "Saul's Jealousy of David." *Envy* typically involves two people, but *jealousy* typically occurs when a third party is added to the mix. Envy is feeling the lack of *something*. Jealousy is feeling threatened by *someone*. Of course, this is not an absolute definition because, to be honest, envy and jealousy most often go hand in hand.

Read 1 Samuel 18:6-9. What happened that turned Saul's envy into jealousy?

Listen, when women are singing about you in the streets, you are praised, but when this is the number one hit in the land (1 Samuel 18:6-7), you are *popular*!

How weird that there seemed to be no reaction from David. Many people might believe that popularity and fame are gifts, but I believe most often they are a test. It seems that just as David was not destroyed by the criticism of his older brother (1 Samuel 17:28), he did not believe his own press. This young man seemed pretty comfortable in his own skin. Could this have been because he spent so much time in solitude? Can we truly get to know ourselves without time in a place where the only conversation is between us and God? David had no other hand to hold. No other person to depend on. No other opinion that matters. It seems David knew his mission.

Wasn't this the very issue with Saul? Along the way, he forgot he was on a mission. He was anointed to lead the people of Israel according to the purposes of God. Yet, instead of keeping his eyes on God and his mission, he allowed the pains, pressures, and comparisons of this world to turn his mission into his identity.

Who are you? Go ahead and make me a list!

Extra Insight

If we live out of an identity based on how God sees us, we no longer feel the need to find our worth in our external circumstances.[26]

Are the things on your list really who you *are*, or are they things you *do*? For example, a few years ago, I would have written wife, mother, and teacher. Yet currently I am no longer a wife, and my job as a mother is different at this stage in my life. If we have placed our identity in the things we do (our missions), then we will come to a place of identity crisis when these things begin to change. Furthermore, if we have made our missions about our identity, then we will take threats or rejection personally. When our missions fail, we will identify ourselves as failures. Brené Brown defines guilt and shame like this: "Shame is a focus on self, guilt is a focus on behavior. Shame is 'I am bad.' Guilt is 'I did something bad.'"[27]

Why is this relevant to our story? Because shame can erode identity. One writer observes, "Both envy and jealousy involve comparisons that reflect a feeling of insufficiency—'I'm inferior to X who has what I want,' or 'I'm inferior to X who may diminish (or is diminishing) my importance to someone.' Feeling 'not enough' is the common thread. Comparisons are a red flag for underlying shame. The greater is the intensity or chronicity of these feelings, the greater shame."[28]

The bottom line? We all hate humiliation!

A great example of this is Cain and Abel (see Genesis 4:1-16). In obedience, Abel approached God with the blood of the innocent sacrifice while Cain brought the fruit of his own labor. He placed on the altar all of the works of his own hand. When they were rejected, Cain was angry. I believe Cain had already connected what he did to who he was—his identity. So, he must have felt rejected! As I read between the lines of Genesis 4:6-7, I hear God assuring him that this isn't so and giving him an opportunity for a "do over."

God seems to be saying, "Cain, you know what is right. Do it!" It's as simple as that. I can imagine the heart of God saying, "You have made the wrong choice, so correct it. This is about what you have done and not who you are. I have rejected your offering. I have not rejected you."

Yet, through eyes of shame, Cain could only see his own rejection and the acceptance of Abel. This humiliation fueled a jealousy that led to murder!

How is the story of Cain and Abel similar to 1 Samuel 18:8-11?

According to verse 12, what was the underlying cause?

Isn't it interesting that verse 12 states it was Saul who was afraid? I would think David would be the one who was afraid, considering a spear with his name on it just flew by his head—*twice*! Yet it was Saul who was afraid, and this fear was fueling an uncontrollable rage.

The sad part for Saul is that all of this inner rage could do nothing to foil the plans of God.

Look at 1 Samuel 18:14-15, and fill in the blanks:

¹⁴"And David had _____ in all his undertakings,

for the LORD was with him. ¹⁵And when Saul saw that he had great

_____, he stood in fearful awe of him."

No matter how much Saul wanted to get rid of David, he had no power to do so. God was in control! No matter how many spears Saul threw, he could not thwart the plans of God. His fight for control was only destroying one person—himself. Didn't both Jonathan and Saul have as much to lose regarding David? Jonathan chose love while Saul chose fear. Jonathan chose to relinquish control to God while Saul chose to fight for control. Jonathan chose to surrender while Saul picked up spears!

What will *you* choose?

Prayer Prompt

Spend some time with your Father, asking Him to reveal the places of insecurity in your life that possibly could be fueling envy or jealousy. Pray for the ability to choose love and form lasting, deep friendships. Ask God to remind you that you are much more than a list of behaviors and that you have intrinsic value as His child. Invite God to show you the areas where you need to surrender and trust Him. And then ask for the strength to put down your spears.

DAY 5

It seems as if the trajectory of David's life was straight up! No matter what Saul attempted to do, David proved successful. But what is truly learned by success?

Today we will cover quite a bit of ground as we watch God begin to remove every comfort from David's life, one by one. I believe David became the man after God's own heart in the shepherd's field, but it would take the wilderness to prepare him to be king.

According to 1 Samuel 18:17-30, whom did David marry?

What was the bride-price required by Saul?

What was the true motive behind this requirement?

What did David actually bring Saul?

Scripture Focus

1 Samuel 18:17-30; 19:18-24; 20:5-34; 21:1-10

David became the man after God's own heart in the shepherd's field, but it would take the wilderness to prepare him to be king.

Am I the only one stunned here? Saul asked for one hundred foreskins and got two hundred. David was the total overachiever, and I bet that just chafed like no other! He was angry and fearful enough to have David killed.

Comfort Removed: Home and Wife

Create a simple timeline below of the major events in 1 Samuel 19:1-18.

This night was the first of many nights David would live as a fugitive. Jonathan's influence on his father was short-lived. Once again, the shame-fueled jealousy of Saul took over, and David had to flee his home and his wife.

Comfort Removed: Samuel

Read 1 Samuel 19:18-21. To where did David flee? And to whom?

What happened to the two different groups of soldiers that Saul sent to capture David?

Close your eyes and imagine this scene. Do you find it funny? Explain your response.

David ran to the very one who anointed him, his spiritual mentor of sorts. David needed guidance, and who better to give it to him than the great prophet Samuel. And let's be honest, everyone knew that Samuel was not a fan of Saul.

Both groups of Saul's soldiers went to Ramah with violence on their minds. Yet when they arrived, Samuel was having "church." The soldiers, moved by the Spirit, began to join in worship. They had come with a job to do, but the Spirit of God had a different plan. Who can argue with the Spirit of God? This powerful person of the Trinity can make people from different nations speak in languages other than their native tongues (Acts 2:1-5), so why couldn't He make these soldiers worship?

Saul could not believe what he was hearing. As the saying goes, "If you need something done right, then do it yourself." So, Saul took off for Ramah.

Now read 1 Samuel 19:22-24. What happened to Saul?

Extra Insights

Maybe Saul thought he was a match for God, but he should have remembered the story of Jacob. After wrestling with God all night and making no progress, Jacob walked away with a new name and a limp. (See Genesis 32:22-32.) Saul didn't even make it to the worship service before he started to prophesy. He began removing his outer, royal garments as a king and humbly appearing as an ordinary man. When he finally reached Naioth, the only thing he could do was bow down.

Who is a match for God? In the New Testament we see that not a storm (Matthew 8:23-27), not a demoniac (Mark 5:1-20), and not even death itself are a match for God (Luke 24:1-12). As the prophet Jeremiah said,

> There is none like you, O Lord;
>   you are great, and your name is great in might.
> (Jeremiah 10:6)

Saul had lost perspective, but this encounter probably reminded him of the power of God. He returned home, but not without being the talk of the town. This story surely stayed alive at dinner tables for years!

As for David, he knew he could not remain in Ramah, so he fled.

Comfort Removed: Jonathan

Having been chased from his home, his wife, and his mentor, David ran back to the person he trusted the most—Jonathan. It is here with Jonathan that we see the emotions of David at their most raw. The two men engaged in some heated words. These were strong, passionate men. David fully and rightfully believed that Saul was trying to kill him, and Jonathan did not. He fully believed in his father. They both had their reasons and arguments, but the bottom line was that they did not agree.

Have you ever strongly disagreed with someone you love? Two people can see the same event or situation so differently. Isn't it amazing how much time two people can waste arguing over the facts of one event? Yet, it happens in

The word for prophesy is *naba'*, and it literally means "to cause to bubble up."[29] It carries the idea of pouring out words. While prophesy can mean to foretell the future, it just as often means to tell forth or speak truth from God as guided by the Holy Spirit.[30]

Naioth was the name of the school of prophets led by Samuel near the town of Ramah, north of Jerusalem. These students were probably Levites who served in the tabernacle and in ceremonial worship there. Groups or schools of prophets are also mentioned in 2 Kings 2:15-18 and 2 Kings 4:38-41.[31]

every relationship, even here with David and Jonathan—two men who loved each other as their own soul.

> I believe the most beautiful verse in this whole story is 1 Samuel 20:4.
> Please write this verse below.

I absolutely love this verse in *The Message*. Jonathan says, "Tell me what you have in mind. I'll do anything for you."

Jonathan realized that arguing over facts or opinions was not getting them anywhere. David was completely rattled. So, Jonathan said the one thing that David needed to hear: "Friend, what do you need from me right now? What can I do to help you?" Isn't that what we all want?

> According to 1 Samuel 20:5-8, what plan did David come up with?

> According to verse 8, had all of David's fears subsided yet?

> Once again Jonathan sought to quiet David's fears. Read 1 Samuel
> 20:11-17, and paraphrase Jonathan's assurances to David in your
> own words.

> What signal would Jonathan send to David about Saul's intentions
> toward David? (vv. 18-23)

According to 1 Samuel 20:24-34, how did Saul react to David's absence? How did this impact Jonathan?

Read 1 Samuel 20:40-42. How do you picture this encounter? Write down your thoughts.

David proved correct about Saul's intentions. Jonathan and David would have to face the gut-wrenching fact that they could no longer be together. Can you feel the intense emotion in verses 40-42? The agony for David must have been greater, considering this was just one more wave of a storm he didn't deserve and seemed unable to escape.

Comfort Removed: Spiritual Community

So often, it is not until we have lost all worldly comforts and end up in the spiritual ditch, so to speak, that we finally look to God. Often that means returning to the people of God for comfort and direction. David sought direction and assistance from the priesthood.

Read 1 Samuel 21:1-10. According to these verses, what caused the high priest to be alarmed upon David's arrival?

Remember, David was a hero. He was highly praised, powerful, and protected. The priest could not understand why this national icon was alone without his honor guard. While we don't know why he lied, David gave a blockbuster-worthy reason why he was alone. He was on an undercover "black op" mission for Saul. This story would cease all inquiries and would explain David's need for haste.

What did David need? (v. 3)

What was the only bread available, according to Ahimelech? (v. 4)

This "uncommon" bread, also called "consecrated bread" (NIV), "holy bread" (ESV), and "sacred bread" (CEV) referred to the twelve loaves of unleavened bread, representing the twelve tribes of Israel, that sat on the Table of Showbread in the Tabernacle. Every Sabbath, they were removed and replaced with twelve new loaves, and the old loaves were given to the priests for food (Leviticus 24:8-9). This bread was referred to as the "bread of the Presence." In Exodus 25:30, the Hebrew word for presence is *paneh*, and it literally means "face."[32] So, in other words, the "bread of the presence" is literally the "bread of the face." That is exactly what it represented, "face to face" fellowship with God.[33] Think about it, when we sit down together to share a meal, we experience face-to-face fellowship.

This same sentiment is expressed in Psalm 27:9, when David describes his longing to feel the presence and fellowship of God:

> *Do not hide your face from me,*
> *do not turn your servant away in anger;*
> *you have been my helper.*
> *Do not reject me or forsake me,*
> *God my Savior.* (NIV)

God may have been removing comforts in David's life, but He was not removing His "face" from him. No matter where David went, the presence of God would go with him.

How about you? Are you feeling alone and distant from the "face" of God? Girlfriend, that is just a feeling. Jesus had that feeling too when He asked, "My God, my God, why hast thou forsaken me?" (Matthew 27:46 KJV). Had God the Father removed His presence from Jesus the Son? Some believe so, but because it is impossible to separate the persons of the Trinity, I affirm with many others that the answer is no. Whether the sin that Jesus bore on the cross caused Him to *feel* distant from God or He was alluding to the full text of the familiar psalm from which He was quoting (Psalm 22), which ends with the sufferer's vindication by God, I believe that the Father never left Him, not for one second. And the same is true for us. God has promised,

"I will never leave you nor forsake you." So we can confidently say,

> *"The Lord is my helper;*
> *I will not fear;*
> *what can man do to me?"*
> (Hebrews 13:5b-6)

Look again at 1 Samuel 21:9. What was the second thing that Ahimelech gave to David?

Wow, talk about a cookie from your "cookie jar." The sword of Goliath—the very sword that would remind David of what the power of God can do when we are faithful. When our eyes betray us, our faith believes in what we cannot see.

I need to highlight one more verse. This verse may seem out of place here, but you will see its importance in the next chapter.

Read 1 Samuel 21:7.

Who was present during this entire exchange between David and Ahimelech?

Who was he?

What was his job and whom did he work for?

Can you say *slave turned spy*?

For the purpose of finishing this storyline, jump ahead with me to 1 Samuel 22. When word got out that David had been spotted in Nob, Saul exploded on his own men for allowing David to once again slip away. He accused them of betraying him and being like his own son Jonathan, who had sided with this rebel David.

Read 1 Samuel 22:6-19. Who decided this was the perfect time to speak up?

What story did he spin?

What happened as a result?

Through word choice, Doeg insinuated that the priests had sided with David and had given him "provisions" and "blessing" for his revolt.

This is the most disgusting scene! Saul had become one of those power-hungry, paranoid dictators who was willing to kill his own people to maintain power. He was willing to use an enemy of Israel to wipe out God's priesthood, and wipe them out he did. He not only had eighty-five priests killed but traveled back to Nob to kill their families as well.

Now read 1 Samuel 22:20-23. How do you think David felt?

David now realized that as a fugitive, anyone who got close to him was in grave danger. I speculate that this is the reason that David's family came to join him in the cave of Adullam (1 Samuel 22:1-2). As long as David was a fugitive, they would not be safe. They too needed a place of hiding. The crowds that David drew were the distressed, indebted, and discontented (1 Samuel 22:2)—some might have thought of them as losers, vagrants, or misfits. Hmmm, sounds familiar. A thousand years later, a distant relative of David from Nazareth would build a kingdom out of the same kinds of people.

What else could possibly be removed from David? Well, next week we will see at least one more thing. But until then, let us close our week by reading all of Psalm 142, which begins,

> ¹With my voice I cry out to the Lord;
> with my voice I plead for mercy to the Lord.
> ²I pour out my complaint before him;
> I tell my trouble before him.

These moving words were penned by David while in the cave of Adullam. See if you can feel his sorrow as you reflect on all he had lost, and then use it as a springboard for your own prayer.

Prayer Prompt

If we have lived long enough, we have lost. Ask your Father to remind you of all that you once may have counted as loss, but now you can see the beauty and growth that came from it. If you are currently in a time of loss, feel free to cry out to your Comforter, like David. He is crying with you today. May God give you the strength to press through.

Fear is often more about the _____ of something than the _____ of it.

The people lost _____. Their fear was affecting their _____.

If you can believe God for the _____, then you can believe Him for the _____.

Every day we have the opportunity to trust God, to _____ our fears. Every day is another chance to be victorious over our _____.

God has _____ you to walk through any battle that comes your way.

This is your fight; fight it with your _____.

Scriptures: 1 Samuel 17, Numbers 13:27-33, 2 Corinthians 5:7, Hebrews 11:1, 1 Kings 18:41-46

Week 5

Control?
Over What?

*Acknowledging We Can't Control
Anything But Ourselves*

(1 Samuel 22–26)

DAY 1

At the conclusion of last week's study, David had lost his home, wife, mentor, and best friend. He was a fugitive, and, therefore, anyone with him or anyone aiding him was in grave danger. We skipped ahead to chapter 22 to see the completed story line, but at this point in chapter 21, the slaughter of the priests at Nob hadn't happened yet—and David had no idea that soon there would be no priesthood to go back to. So, with bread and sword in hand, he desperately needed somewhere to hide.

Read 1 Samuel 21:10-15. Where did David choose to flee?

Who recognized David?

According to verses 12 and 13, what did David do once he realized he had been recognized, and why?

David was a fugitive. What better place to "get lost" than in the large Philistine city of Gath, Goliath's hometown? Who in the world would look for David there? To put it in a modern context, we might imagine him walking the city streets in a black hoodie, sleeping in a ratty hotel room, and avoiding all human contact. Yet, even then someone recognized him. The servants of Achish couldn't believe their eyes. David, the future king of Israel, in Gath? That's crazy!

Scripture Focus

1 Samuel 21:10-15;
22:1, 6-23

Extra Insight

In 2019, archaeologists uncovered evidence that the biblical city of Gath was large, covering an area of almost 125 acres—more than twice the size of most other towns at the time. It was comparable to Jerusalem at its height a few hundred years later.[1]

Yep. David ran with the insanity angle, pretending to be out of his mind. He started scrawling on the city gates and drooling into his beard, which was so undignified that only a madman would allow it in that culture.[2]

This once hero appeared to have gone insane.

I don't know about you, but there have been days I could have worked this angle really well. I've had days when I was on the edge of banging my head against a wall in an attempt to get everyone to leave me alone! Yet the servants didn't risk it, and they took David to the king.

Look again at verses 14-15. What was Achish's response?

Achish basically said, "What am I running here, an asylum? Don't I have enough people not in their right minds? Do I need another? Obviously, this man is no longer a threat to us. Get him out of here." I cannot help but wonder if Achish wanted them to let David go or to kill him. These Philistine soldiers had the "giant killer" in their grasp! Oh, the things they must have dreamed of doing to David.

David departed from there and escaped to the cave of Adullam. And when his brothers and all his father's house heard it, they went down there to him.

(1 Samuel 22:1)

Read 1 Samuel 22:1 in the margin, and write the two verbs from the first sentence below.

Which word do you think fits the scene better? Why?

Where did David go?

With nowhere to go, David ended up in the cave of Adullam where he penned Psalm 142. Oh, how this psalm gives us insight into the emotions of David during this time. It is here that he found out about the slaughter at Nob.

Read Psalm 142:4 in the margin. Have you ever felt like this? Have you ever thought to yourself "no one cares for my soul"? If so, describe that time briefly below.

Look to the right and see:
there is none who takes
notice of me;
no refuge remains to me;
no one cares for
my soul.

(Psalm 142:4)

When those dark times come, it's hard not to question God. *God, what are you doing? Why are you allowing this? What do you want from me? Whose side are you on?*

When the wheels of life are coming off and we have no control, we are forced to face our true beliefs about God. Is He in control? Does He truly love me? Is He good? How can a good God allow so much pain?

How *can* a good God allow an entire priesthood to be slaughtered? Let's explore this.

Review 1 Samuel 22:6-23, which we read on Day 5 of last week.
According to verse 16, who ordered the slaughter?

King Saul ordered the executions freely out of the evil in his own heart. Remember, he didn't start out as a monster. His decline was a downward spiral. He started like many people: young, passionate, insecure, and fearful. But as his success grew, he failed to recognize the blinding ego growing within him. Perhaps he felt criticized, rejected, misunderstood, and unappreciated, becoming the victim! It's likely that he allowed envy, shame, and jealousy to reign, producing a hatred that led to mass murder. This can happen to any of us when our egos are allowed to reign.

Although Saul killed the priests of Nob out of his own free will, this atrocity did not happen outside of God's sovereign purpose, because God used it to fulfill a prior judgment on Eli and his sons.

Read 1 Samuel 2:30-31. What had God said would happen to the house of Eli?

How do we reconcile an evil act of free will that played into a purpose that was determined fifty years before? The early Christians were faced with this same dilemma.

Read Acts 2:22-23 in the margin. According to these verses, who crucified Jesus? Was God surprised?

It was God's plan for Jesus to die for our sins, but we must not blame God! This was the choice of human beings—in a sense, a decision we all share, because we are no different than the people of Jesus's day. God did not force this action. They did what was in their hearts. And we do the same.

When we human beings are given a chance, we will betray and even murder our Maker. Yet do not think that we have the power to do anything outside the will of God! So, who can truly understand the sovereignty of God and the free will of humanity? No one. It is mystery.

We will never understand some events this side of eternity. Why do bad things happen to good people? What things have been foreseen by God that will play out in our present-day lives by our own and others' free will? These thoughts are too much for me to grasp. When I cannot fathom what God is doing in the midst of what is happening, I choose to rely on His goodness.

Instead of asking God, "Why is this happening to me?" I am learning to ask, "How is this happening for me?" In other words, how can I grow from this event? I claim verses such as Jeremiah 29:11 and Romans 8:28.

Read Jeremiah 29:11 and Romans 8:28 in the margin. What assurance do these verses give us?

There have been many days over the past two years when I, like David, have felt the loneliness of the cave—mourning over all of my losses, blaming myself for the pain of others, and questioning the purposes of God. I too have felt like an outcast—rejected, misunderstood, and falsely blamed. Yet, unlike David, I did not pen any psalms. Instead, the mountain trails of Phoenix heard my laments. My tears, mixed with sweat, ran down my face as I cried out, "God is in control, He is good, and He loves me!" I held on to those simple truths like a life preserver as the waves of panic swelled. To be honest, that's all I could do for a while. The words *hope* and *future* were not even in my vocabulary. But when I finally had the strength to stand and sort through the rubble, I realized my foundation was still there. That is when the rebuilding started.

At that point the cup had already spilled, which gave me the freedom to stop controlling an outward image and start growing a soul! My divorce did not take God by surprise. He watched with compassion when I spun out of control initially. He listened with understanding as I questioned everything I believed. And He smiled with excitement as I began to open up and bloom. *How could God use even this*, I wondered, *to chip away at my veneer and bring about true authenticity*?

That question led to other questions. How can we truly lead if we don't understand suffering? How can we truly have compassion if we don't know pain? How can we truly know ourselves if we are not left alone in the dark? How can we understand humility if we haven't been humbled?

I do not believe for one moment that it was God's will for me to be divorced, but He allowed it. The blame is shared between two broken people. Yet, I do believe that God can use it for my good and for His ultimate glory.

Charles Swindoll writes this about David:

> David has been brought to the place God can truly begin to shape him and use him. When the sovereign God brings us to nothing, it is to reroute our lives, not to end them. Human perspective says, "Aha, you've lost this, you've lost that. You've caused this, you've caused that. You've ruined this, you've ruined that. End your life!" But God says, "No. No. You're in the cave. But that doesn't mean it's curtains. That means it's time to reroute your life. Now's the time to start anew!" That's exactly what he does with David.[3]

What David needed right then was a halftime speech—you know, that speech that says, "We may be down, but we are not out! I know you're tired, but suck it up. This is what we have trained for! There is more in the tank than you think!"

David was not alone, and neither are we. We are part of an amazing team! If you would like to see part of the roster, turn to Hebrews 11. The names in that chapter made it to the hall of fame. If you take the time to go back and read their stories, you will discover that they too experienced failure, isolation, doubt, and suffering. Yet they stayed in the fight. They did not give up. What's more, those superstars, along with multitudes of others, are in the stands watching you and cheering you on.

Read Hebrews 12:1-2 in the margin. How do you feel knowing that you are surrounded by a "cloud of witnesses"?

> # When I cannot fathom what God is doing in the midst of what is happening, I choose to rely on His goodness.

[1]Therefore, since we are surrounded by so great a cloud of witnesses, let us also lay aside every weight, and sin which clings so closely, and let us run with endurance the race that is set before us, [2]looking to Jesus, the founder and perfecter of our faith, who for the joy that was set before him endured the cross, despising the shame, and is seated at the right hand of the throne of God.
(Hebrews 12:1-2)

This is not a beautiful white cloud you look up and see in the sky; it is an all-encompassing cloud that you can feel. The Hebrew word here for *surrounded* means "encompassing, encircled, and embraced."[4] This cloud of witnesses is encircling you, embracing you. You are not alone! They have been there. They too have fought the fight. They know what it takes, and they know you have it. Can you hear the roar of this amazing crowd?

Finish your time today by turning to Hebrews 11. Review this list of your teammates and their stories. Allow their cheers to encourage you to stay in the fight!

Prayer Prompt

As you spend time in Hebrews 11, ask God to give you insights into the men and women listed there. What was different, unique, or even common about them? How did God use them? How did God reveal Himself to and through them? But don't just learn from the saints of the past. Also talk with God about some current day saints you know—living, breathing people in your own faith community. What about their stories or their witness has encouraged or inspired you? How have they spurred you on to continue the race?

DAY 2

Scripture Focus

1 Samuel 23:1-18

No matter how much we may want to stay in the cave, life has a way of moving on, and so must we. The cave is a place to reroute, not a place to relocate. There is one thing I have learned from being in the cave: you truly find out who your people are! While in the cave, David accumulated a motley crew: "everyone who was in distress, and everyone who was in debt, and everyone who was bitter in soul" (1 Samuel 22:2)—a group of misfits who later would become the "mighty men" of David (see also 2 Samuel 23:8-39 and 1 Chronicles 11:10-47).

David and his men were now living in the forest of Hereth in the land of Judah. This sounds a little bit like Robin Hood, doesn't it? In some ways it was. In our story we have an "evil" king (Saul) who was obsessed with finding his so-called enemy (David). This enemy, surrounded by his loyal but motley crew, seemed to care about the people more than the king did. While Saul spent his time obsessing over finding David, his own people were being attacked by the Philistines.

Read 1 Samuel 23:1-5. What was troubling David, and what did he do?

When David found out that the Philistines were attacking and looting the people of Keilah, obviously he was compelled to help. He was a warrior. He was not used to sitting on the sidelines. Yet he understood who was actually calling the plays, so he inquired of God.

Man, can we learn from David! Just because we are moved in our hearts doesn't mean we are called to act. Every cause is not *our* cause. Every battle is not *our* battle. We are not the answer to every problem. Just because we *can* doesn't mean we *should*. We need to seek wisdom.

I can think of some good reasons David should not engage in this battle. How about you? Write any ideas below.

Extra Insight

Courage without wisdom is just brave acts of stupid!
—Steph Redhead[5]

What David might have listed:

- The timing isn't good for me.
- My army is not in tip-top shape.
- I am personally not in a good place.
- The last thing I need is another enemy.
- I need to pick my battles.
- This would expose me to Saul.

What did God tell David to do? (v. 2)

How did David's men feel about this? (v. 3)

I think David's men thought he had lost his ever-loving mind! "Dude, we are hiding in a forest. Our own king is trying to kill us, and now you want us to expose ourselves not only to him but to take on the Philistines, too?" I'm with them. This made absolutely no sense!

How did David respond? (v. 4)

Extra Insight

Without courage wisdom bears no fruit.
—Baltasar Gracian[6]

Hey, the guys had a point. There is nothing wrong with getting assurance, especially when the action doesn't seem wise on the surface. David made sure this was not about him and something he needed, and instead what God wanted.

David returned with the same answer: "Mount up!" Do you think David's men saw it—that sparkle in his eye? That confident resolve? The scales of depression had fallen away, and once again David remembered who he was—the giant killer. The future king of Israel. Who could argue with that? Not his men, and not the Philistines.

What were the results of the battle? (v. 5)

It's amazing what can happen when we get our eyes off of ourselves and onto others.

Attempting to rescue the town of Keilah made no sense from a human perspective. Was God actually going to use David, a fugitive, to free His people? Yet, who better to fight for your freedom then someone who knew what it was like not to have it? The best leaders are those who can empathize.

Isn't it good to see David back on the field doing what God had created him to do? It's amazing what can happen when we get our eyes off of ourselves and onto others.

I cannot begin to tell you how many times over the past two years I have wanted to quit teaching. The unrelenting arrows of self-pity, insecurity, fear, and judgment seemed too numerous to outmaneuver at times. But I didn't quit! If I'm being honest, many days I just walked through the motions. I taught because that is what I do. I'm not sure if it was out of obedience or obligation, but I just kept teaching. Yet, somewhere along the way, that spark returned, and everyone saw it. A raw, vulnerable Shannon was bursting forth.

I began to recognize a familiar pain in others, and I was determined to cheer on my sisters who were in the cave, shouting out that halftime speech, encouraging them to live a more authentic life—to be who God created them to be; to quit trying to control a narrative and instead allow God to use their brokenness to rescue others. I wanted them to know that they were stronger than they thought they were, that they were not alone, that the Spirit of the

Living God was dwelling in them! God actually increased my passion and influence through my brokenness.

Read Matthew 16:25 in the margin. What does this say about brokenness and loss leading to life?

"For whoever wants to save their life will lose it, but whoever loses their life for me will find it."
(Matthew 16:25 NIV)

Through my brokenness, I got my fight back! I wish Nichole Nordeman knew how many times I sang the lyrics to her song, "Sound of Surviving," shouting from the mountaintops of Phoenix that, "I'm not done fighting / This is the sound of surviving."[7]

Read 1 Samuel 23:6-8. What assumption does Saul make?

Was God really leading David into Saul's hand? Knowing the complete story, we can confidently say no. Yet this was Saul's perception.

How often in real life do we analyze our circumstances in an attempt to understand God? When bad things happen, we say, "Why is God doing this to me?" When good things happen, we say, "Thank you, God, for coming through." When Pharaoh let the people go, they rejoiced at what God had done. Yet, at the edge of the Red Sea, they accused Him of sending them out into the desert to die. We are so shortsighted.

With false confidence, Saul called all the forces together for battle, to go to Keilah and besiege David and his men. Instead of going to protect Keilah from the Philistines, Saul was coming to attack them and acquire David. How many of his own people had to die so Saul could apprehend his perceived enemy? What had happened to Saul? Where is the compassion he once felt for his people? How did Saul's judgment become so skewed?

The question for us is, how do we make sure we do not confuse our perception with reality? Meditate on the following verses and write any insights below each.

The way of a fool is right in his own eyes,
but a wise man listens to advice.
(Proverbs 12:15)

Finally, brothers, whatever is true, whatever is honorable, whatever is just, whatever is pure, whatever is lovely, whatever is commendable, if there is any excellence, if there is anything worthy of praise, think about these things.

(Philippians 4:8)

Count it all joy, my brothers, when you meet trials of various kinds, for you know that the testing of your faith produces steadfastness.

(James 1:2-3)

And my God will supply every need of yours according to his riches in glory in Christ Jesus.

(Philippians 4:19)

Now read 1 Samuel 23:9-14. What did David do when he got wind of Saul's plan?

Unlike Saul, David did not count on perception. He needed reality—God's reality. So, he called the high priest over with his ephod containing the Urim and Thummim (see page 54) and began to inquire of God. The reality was that Saul was coming for him, and in the end the people of Keilah would turn him over.

I cannot imagine how David felt when he realized that the very people he had saved from the Philistines would turn him over to his enemy. I wonder if he felt angry, resentful, or even sorry for himself. Have you ever fallen into those emotions, frustrated that you were the first person to help but, in the end, others took advantage of you? I think Jesus would have a lot to say about that!

We aren't told how David felt; we're only told what he did in response to Saul's plans. He retreated. He refused to allow his problem to become the problem for everyone else. David was not one to run from a fight, but he was not willing to watch innocent men die in a battle that wasn't theirs. David knew when to fight and when to retreat.

Moving from one place to the next, David tried to stay just out of reach of Saul and his many spies. This had to get so old, right? They had to be exhausted. Eventually he led his men into the Wilderness of Ziph, a town south of the Dead Sea with a diverse landscape, including rocky crags, hills, valleys, and arid terrain.[8] This is not a place you'd choose for a vacation. Yet, God was with David. He was guiding and protecting him, but it wasn't comfortable.

Do you ever feel like you are only one misstep away from disaster? One paycheck away from bankruptcy? One missed rent payment away from homelessness? Do you ever wonder when God is going to give you a break, give you some margin, give you some comfort? Do you ever question the fairness of life? Do you ever wonder "Why me?" Especially when others seem to be doing so well? I know I do!

Yet I have to believe that God is doing something. I would love to interview David and ask him what he learned during those very uncomfortable days. Maybe that should be our assignment today. Take some time to call someone or go to coffee with someone who has been through trials. Ask them what they learned and what these trials produced in them. Don't just take it from David; ask a current-day saint for encouragement so that you can stand in your trial. During times like these, we all need encouragement!

During this time, God did not give David freedom from his trial, but He did give David an amazing friend. Look who showed up.

Read 1 Samuel 23:15-18. According to verse 16, what did Jonathan do?

Jonathan could not rescue David. He could not fix David's problem. He didn't have all the answers. But what Jonathan did have were the promises of God. He reminded David that he had nothing to fear. In so many words, he told David, "God will protect you. You will become king. You are not alone; I am with you!" In my darkest moments, God has always been faithful to provide for me—one or many friends who come and sit in my presence, knowing there is nothing they can do to fix my broken heart. Unwilling to leave me alone in my pain, they sit in quiet resolve until the moment God places one promise on their tongue just for me. My prayer is for you to have those kinds of friends, too.

Prayer Prompt

Spend some time in prayer today thanking God for this kind of friend. If none comes to your mind, ask God to help you cultivate that kind of friendship. Finally, ask God who could really use that kind of friend today, and reach out to that person!

DAY 3

Scripture Focus

1 Samuel 23:19-29;
24:1-22

Yesterday we left David in the Desert of Ziph with his friend Jonathan, and today we see that David barely made it out of the land alive. Let's pick up where we left off.

Read 1 Samuel 23:19-29.

How many times in this passage did Saul track David down?

What happened that finally allowed David to escape Saul?

Saul was literally breathing down David's neck when the word came that the Philistines were attacking Israel. Saul had to cease pursuing David and go fight an actual enemy. David and his men used this time to escape to the region of Engedi.

Engedi was an oasis in the desert. It has a temperate climate and is the site of one of only two freshwater springs on the western shore of the Dead Sea.[9] This spring begins 656 feet above the Dead Sea, producing a powerful waterfall. It is known for its diverse foliage and abundant wildlife. The name Engedi actually means the "spring of the goat." During biblical days, it was known for its date palm trees and abundance of balsam, a plant used for making perfume.[10]

Having visited there, I can tell you Engedi is like a breath of fresh air. It is a hidden jewel tucked into a vast barren wilderness. It is a place that draws you in with all of your senses.

Read Psalm 63 below and imagine all that was around David in this natural oasis. With every sense aroused, he was breathing in the

presence of God. Underline key words and phrases that reflect the environment around David.

¹God—you're my God!

I can't get enough of you!

I've worked up such hunger and thirst for God,

traveling across dry and weary deserts.

²⁻⁴So here I am in the place of worship, eyes open,

drinking in your strength and glory.

In your generous love I am really living at last!

My lips brim praises like fountains.

I bless you every time I take a breath;

My arms wave like banners of praise to you.

⁵⁻⁸I eat my fill of prime rib and gravy;

I smack my lips. It's time to shout praises!

If I'm sleepless at midnight,

I spend the hours in grateful reflection.

Because you've always stood up for me,

I'm free to run and play.

I hold on to you for dear life,

and you hold me steady as a post.

⁹⁻¹¹Those who are out to get me are marked for doom,

marked for death, bound for hell.

They'll die violent deaths;

jackals will tear them limb from limb.

But the king is glad in God;

his true friends spread the joy,

While small-minded gossips

are gagged for good.

(Psalm 63 MSG)

As David penned the words "God—you're my God! I can't get enough of you! I've worked up such hunger and thirst for God, traveling across dry and weary deserts," can't you just imagine how thirsty he and his men were when they finally made it across the barren wilderness to this freshwater spring at Engedi? David was telling God that his thirst for Him was even greater.

Extra Insight

Many believe that David wrote Psalm 63 while in a cave in Engedi.[11]

In verses 2-4 of Psalm 63, I can see David gazing into the starlit sky. Psalm 19:1 says, "The heavens declare the glory of God; / the skies proclaim the work of his hands" (NIV). No wonder David referred to this as a great place of worship. Instead of the sound of a choir, the roaring spring could be heard throughout the canyon. Oh, how David thanked God for this unlimited refreshment in a dry, parched land. Can't you just hear him take a much-needed deep breath? As he saw the date palms wave their branches in the wind, David lifted his hands to praise his Creator.

What insights can you gain from Psalm 63:5-8?

This spring brought in a variety of animals for their culinary delight. This was a place to replenish. I just wonder if, in the cool of the night when David could not sleep, he ever watched the animals play by the springs in the moonlight. This oasis allowed David to rejuvenate and to reflect.

Extra Insight

Ecotherapy, also known as green therapy or nature therapy, connects people with the outdoors to promote healing and personal growth. This interaction aids in dealing with physical and mental illnesses.[12]

Not only was the watering hole a good place to see animals play, but it also was a place where one might see the violence of the circle of life. How might this have played into David's words in verses 9-11?

David's time in Engedi makes me think about a growing scientific field called ecotherapy (see Extra Insight), which has shown great connection between time spent in nature and the decrease of stress, anxiety, and depression. One experiment compared healthy people sent on a ninety-minute walk, some out in nature, and others in an urban area. The findings are fascinating:

> [T]hose who did a nature walk had lower activity in the prefrontal cortex, a brain region that is active during rumination—defined as repetitive thoughts that focus on negative emotions.

> "When people are depressed or under high levels of stress, this part of the brain malfunctions, and people experience a continuous loop of negative thoughts," says Dr. Strauss.[13]

Dr. Jason Strauss went on to say that even the sounds of nature have a calming effect. Both nature sounds and outdoor silence have a calming effect, lowering blood pressure and cortisol, the stress hormone. He noted that even the visual aspects of nature can soothe us, saying, "Having something pleasant to focus on like trees and greenery helps distract your mind from negative thinking, so your thoughts become less filled with worry."[14]

While some may find this baffling, I do not. God made us to be a part of nature. He created us to have our feet in the soil and our lungs filled with fresh air, to see and experience the awesomeness of His creation. We are wired for it!

Personally, I feel so much closer to God when I am out in His beautiful creation. When I am sitting on the top of a mountain looking out at the vast desert below and the many mountain ranges in the distance, I am reminded of the enormity of my God. He is powerful, creative, and beautiful. When up there, the world's problems seem much smaller in comparison. You don't have to be an extreme outdoors person to experience this. Go to the park or anywhere you can put your feet in some grass and see a beautiful tree waving in the wind.

Recall a time when you were able to go outside and spend time meditating on God or Scripture, breathing in deeply, and syncing your soul to the rhythms of creation. Write some reflections below about that time. How did it help you to feel closer to God? (You'll be encouraged to take time for a similar experience at the end of today's lesson.)

God made us to be a part of nature. He created us to have our feet in the soil and our lungs filled with fresh air, to see and experience the awesomeness of His creation.

Okay, back to our story. Thanks to the Philistines, David enjoyed a short reprieve from Saul. But just like every good vacation, this too would come to an end.

Read 1 Samuel 24:1-7. What did David's men assume regarding this coincidental encounter?

What did David's men want him to do?

What did he do instead?

Wow, talk about getting caught with your pants down! Can you believe it? Of all the caves in the world to stop and enjoy the "Israelite Times," Saul stopped in this one—the very cave David and his men were hiding in.

David could have easily taken Saul's life right there in that cave. His men sure wanted him to! They fully believed that this was the way God would fulfill His promise to David by making him the next king of Israel. Yet, ponder this with me for a minute.

If David had killed the reigning king of Israel, how do you think things would have played out? Journal your thoughts below.

How do you think the nation would have responded to the assassination of their king? Wouldn't David have just been playing into what Saul had said about him all along? What position would Jonathan have been put in? Once you had killed the king, there would be no coming back from that! Oh, the messes we create when we step out from under the timing of God and take things into our own hands.

The time in Engedi served David well. He had time to think, breathe, and replenish, to see the Creator's hand at work and to remember that he could trust it!

Why do you think David cut off a corner of Saul's robe?

Here, clothing is not an element of deception, as it was for Jacob and Joseph (see Week 2). Instead, it is a symbol of status and rank. Saul's robe represented his status as the king of Israel.

One source notes that, in the ancient world, "The hem of the outer robe was ornate compared to the rest of it. The more important the individual, the more elaborate the hem's embroidery. Its significance lies not in its artistry but in its symbolism, as an extension of its owner's person and authority."[15] Therefore, Saul's hem represented his person and authority as king. David did not kill Saul, but symbolically dethroned him.

How did David feel after cutting Saul's hem? Why? (vv. 5-6)

Who was David that he should take it upon himself to remove God's king? Saul was God's anointed, and if Saul was to be removed, God would do that Himself. What precedent would be set if David, a mere man, chose to make such a decision? Would he then be any different than Saul? If David was going to be a good king, he must understand and follow the chain of command.

Read 1 Samuel 24:8-15, and paraphrase these verses in your own words below. Put yourself in David's shoes, considering all that he had lost.

Remember his time in the cave. Imagine his natural desire to defend himself and the anger he felt having been unjustly accused. Do you hear the desperation in his voice as he pleaded with Saul to be logical and reasonable?

Now read 1 Samuel 24:16-22. What do you think about Saul's response?

Compare 1 Samuel 24:20 and 1 Samuel 15:26-29 in the margin. What similarities do you see? What connections can you make?

The picture is coming together, isn't it? I am sure when David held up the hem of Saul's robe, Saul remembered this scene with Samuel. Holy flashbacks, Batman! In his desperate attempt to control and maintain power, Saul had disrespected the old prophet. He ripped his hem. He challenged his authority. Yet his control had accomplished nothing. The prophet's words were coming true before his very eyes. David had stripped the kingdom from him, if only symbolically for now.

How often have our own attempts to control accomplished nothing? When we are tempted to take control, may we remember this scene between

"And now, behold, I know that you shall surely be king, and that the kingdom of Israel shall be established in your hand."
(1 Samuel 24:20)

26And Samuel said to Saul, "I will not return with you. For you have rejected the word of the LORD, and the LORD has rejected you from being king over Israel." 27As Samuel turned to go away, Saul seized the skirt of his robe, and it tore. 28And Samuel said to him, "The LORD has torn the kingdom of Israel from you this day and has given it to a neighbor of yours, who is better than you. 29And also the Glory of Israel will not lie or have regret, for he is not a man, that he should have regret."
(1 Samuel 15:26-29)

Saul and David and ask God to help us have an attitude of humility, respect, and patience.

Prayer Prompt

Today we saw that David needed time to think, breathe, and replenish. We need those times too. I encourage you to end your time today with just that kind of experience. If possible, go outside and take a literal stroll with your heavenly Father, breathing in deeply! (If that's not possible, take an imaginative stroll in your mind's eye.) Now, do whatever you feel led to do—whatever you need to replenish your soul. God simply wants to meet with you today. He loves you as you are—whether you have praises on your lips or bitterness in your bones. You can trust Him with either, even when life seems completely out of control. Because even then, God is never out of control.

DAY 4

Scripture Focus

1 Samuel 25

We ended our study yesterday with a piece of Saul's hem missing and the words of Samuel ringing in his ears. Today we hear the sound of mourning as the nation says goodbye to Samuel, the great prophet.

Read 1 Samuel 25:1. What national event was happening in Israel?

This single verse dedicated to the death of Samuel almost seems like a sidebar. If someone were telling this story, I can hear them saying, "Oh yeah, and by the way, Samuel died." Yet we know it is significant because all of Israel assembled and mourned. I believe this one verse sets the tone for the entire chapter.

Samuel's death and national funeral not only gave David and his men some moving room, allowing them to travel about more freely because Saul and his men were busy, but it also gave some clues to David's state of mind in this chapter.

How do you think David was feeling upon receiving the news about Samuel? (Dig deeper than just "sad" as you think of all that was going on at this event.)

Extra Insight

The Bible does not specifically state how soon a person was buried after death, but it likely took place within a day. This was due to the climate and because Israelites did not embalm the dead and did not practice cremation.[16]

I am sure David took the news of Samuel's death pretty hard. Samuel was the one who had anointed David, speaking into his life the purposes and promises of God. Samuel was the one who had protected and encouraged David in his great time of need when he initially fled from Saul. Samuel was a living reminder of God's faithfulness, and now he was gone. David was not able to say goodbye or even give his respects.

Everyone had assembled to honor someone David loved and respected, and he couldn't be there with them. The world was moving forward without him, and there was nothing David could do to change it. I wonder if he allowed his mind to imagine all the people who were present, all the stories that were told, and all the tears that were shared. Did he wonder if the mourners thought of him or, more important, *what* they thought of him? Was he so easily forgotten? Did they ever care for him at all? It is very hard being on the outside.

I can relate to that. I can understand being part of a family for twenty-five years and then, in one moment, "dying" to them. The problem is, I didn't actually die. I watched at a distance as their lives moved on exactly as they always had—the same people, same trips, and same stories. The only difference was that I was now "out."

When you are on the outside, all sorts of questions plague your mind. *Does anyone miss me? Do they ever think of me? What do they think of me? Was every gesture of affection genuine?* When you are the one on the outside, insecurity has a way of making everything seem to be about you. Rejection hurts, and it can fuel powerful anger if you are not careful.

Describe a time when you felt rejected or left out. What thoughts and emotions did you experience? How did you heal—or have you?

> **Rejection hurts, and it can fuel powerful anger if you are not careful.**

All of this, I believe, formed the undercurrent for the events of chapter 25. David surely felt rejected and wounded by his own people. The last thing he likely would endure now was the rejection and insult of a foolish man. With this backdrop, let's dive in.

*The fear of the LORD is the
beginning of knowledge;
fools despise wisdom
and instruction.*
(Proverbs 1:7)

———————

*⁸Do not reprove a scoffer,
or he will hate you;
reprove a wise man,
and he will love you.
⁹Give instruction to a wise
man, and he will be still
wiser;
teach a righteous man,
and he will increase in
learning.
¹⁰The fear of the LORD is the
beginning of wisdom,
and the knowledge of
the Holy One is insight.*
(Proverbs 9:8-10)

Read 1 Samuel 25:1-3, and circle any words below used to describe Nabal:

Rich	Kind	Harsh
Handsome	Prudent	Badly behaved

Now circle any words below used to describe Abigail:

Nagging	Beautiful	Fearful
Discerning	Foolish	Stubborn

Allow me to give you one more very important piece of information about Nabal. His name actually means "fool." When we view this with help from the Proverbs, we begin to get a much clearer picture of Nabal.

Read Proverbs 1:7 and Proverbs 9:8-10 in the margin. What do these verses reveal about a fool such as Nabal?

*¹⁰Who can find a virtuous
wife?
For her worth is far above
rubies.
¹¹The heart of her
husband safely trusts her;
So he will have no lack
of gain.
¹²She does him good
and not evil
All the days of her life.*
(Proverbs 31:10-12 NKJV)

Although Nabal was very rich according to the world's standards, he failed to recognize that the greatest thing he lacked was wisdom. Well, one can only acquire that in proper perspective with God. Nabal was an arrogant man, a fool who refused instruction, allowing his wealth to deceive him into thinking he held a position of power.

Nabal failed to recognize what he *lacked*, and we will see that he also failed to recognize what he *had*. The greatest thing he had was a godly wife—worth far more than jewels (see margin).

Not only did Nabal marry a wife of great wisdom, but she was also rolled up in a beautiful package! Oh, and how I love that the narrator mentioned her wisdom before her beauty, because Proverbs 31:30 reminds us that beauty is fleeting but wisdom remains. If you are close to my age, you are experiencing this on the daily! There is not enough Botox in the world to completely stop the aging process, but while our bodies decline, I pray our wisdom increases.

Abigail's name means "My Father Is Joy" or "The Father Is Joyful."[17] What an example of a truly strong, wise, and beautiful woman in Scripture!

According to 1 Samuel 25:4, what was the occasion for which David sent his servants to talk with Nabal?

Extra Insight

Sheep shearing took place in the spring months, and it was done by either the owners or professional shearers. Shearing was detailed work with the goal of keeping the fleece whole.[18]

The time for shearing sheep was a great occasion. Families would come together for great feasts celebrating the harvest of wool. This was a time of thanksgiving that should have been accompanied by an attitude of gratitude and giving. In his book on David, Charles Swindoll writes that at the time of sheep shearing, it was customary to set aside a portion of the profit for those who had helped protect the owner's sheep—sort of like the unwritten rule of a tip.[19] This should have been an atmosphere of celebration and generosity.

Now read 1 Samuel 25:5-8. What did David ask his men to do?

Give two examples of humility in their request.

David did not presume. He did not demand. He spoke blessings on Nabal and humbly asked Nabal to share his blessing. It stood to reason that Nabal would show his gratitude by supplying David and his men with some good provisions. After all, Nabal was already an incredibly wealthy man!

Read 1 Samuel 25:9-11, and write below what you think Nabal's response would sound like in today's language. (Read *The Message* version if you need a little help.)

Here's my modern-day paraphrase: "Who is David? Who is this son of Jesse? His name holds no power here. This land is full of runaway servants! As far as you guys, I can't begin to think of where you are from or where you have been. Give you my food? No way. I don't even want you in my presence."

Can't you imagine this arrogant man taking a bite out of his lamb chop and insulting David's men? He probably had a greasy right-hand man beside him laughing at every antagonistic comment.

Read 1 Samuel 25:12-13. What did David's men do, and how did David respond?

Humiliated, the men returned to David and they did not leave out one single word of Nabal's insults. No sooner had the words come out of their mouths than David yelled, "Load up!" With everyone packing—and I'm not talking about luggage here—they headed off to kick butt and take names. If we really want to know how David was feeling, we can skip ahead a few verses and eavesdrop on his rant with his soldiers.

Read 1 Samuel 25:21-22, and write David's rant in your own words below.

David lost it! The behavior of this fool Nabal was the straw that broke the camel's back. At the beginning of our lesson today, I suggested to you the many feelings David might have been experiencing as a result of Samuel's death. Well, I believe Nabal turned the heat up one too many notches and David was about to blow. It's one thing to run from the king. At least he had been given the respect of a worthy opponent. But to be insulted by this fool and treated like he was totally insignificant? Well, that was a whole other thing!

David needed help in order to not act foolishly like Nabal!

Read 1 Samuel 25:23-27.

Who acted quickly to help?

How did Abigail find out about the situation, and what did she do?

These verses show us a great lesson! To be a person of wisdom, we need to be approachable. The servant must have known that Abigail was a woman of reason and not just emotion. Surely he came to her because she would listen and know what to do. Perhaps she had had a lot of practice putting out fires considering the "fool" she was married to. She probably had ample experience staying one step ahead of the potential disasters her husband created. My guess is that this wasn't the first time her family needed her to save them from Nabal's rash behavior.

Not only was Abigail cool, calm, and collected, but she also was prepared. She rushed out with abundant provisions for David and his men. Some would argue that she disobeyed her husband. I would argue that she saved him. She saved Nabal, along with the whole family, from his foolishness. Sometimes love is tough!

Abigail arrived just in time to hear David's rant. If there was one thing she was good at, it was talking a ranting man off the ledge.

Read 1 Samuel 25:28-31. What points did Abigail make to David? What did she remind him of?

Abigail did what any good crisis intervention counselor would do. She convinced David to calm down, focus on her, and talk. She told David she understood his frustration, and that if anyone comprehended the absolute irritation of Nabal, she did! While providing for David's needs, she reminded him what he had to live for. God had promised to establish David's kingdom, and in relation to that, who was Nabal?

Read 1 Samuel 25:32-35. How did David respond to Abigail?

The wise words of this woman on that day saved not only her family but also her future king! David had allowed emotion to carry him into a situation he didn't need to be in. Slaughtering Nabal was not something David wanted on his conscience. He had many battles coming in the future, but this was not one of them. The anger he was feeling inside went much deeper than Nabal.

How might this event have been preparing David to be king?

I am sure David would never forget this amazing woman, and she would not forget David. Perhaps she felt that finally a man had listened to her.

Finally, a man recognized her wisdom and actually heeded her words. Finally she was appreciated. This was a cookie jar moment.

When she returned home, she found her husband in a drunken frenzy, so she kept her actions a secret until the next morning. Again, wise woman!

Read 1 Samuel 25:36-43. What happened to Nabal when Abigail finally shared the details of what she had done? Write your thoughts here. I know you have some good ones!

When David found out that Nabal had died, what did he do?

> May we always be willing to listen to the voices of wisdom in our own lives, especially when our emotions leave us off kilter.

Hey, David was no dummy. He knew a good woman when he saw one!

When fate seemed to serve Saul up on a silver platter in the cave that day, David followed God, not his emotions. Yet, in a moment of personal grief, he could not hold back the waves that were pushing him to the shores of regret. His emotions were too raw, too fresh, and too close to the surface when he encountered Nabal. No one is perfect. Thank God for the wisdom of Abigail, and thank God for David's willingness to listen.

Like David, may we always be willing to listen to the voices of wisdom in our own lives, especially when our emotions leave us off kilter.

Prayer Prompt

Spend some time in a quiet place today, listening to your emotions. What is going on inside? Are you sad, hurt, mad? Ask God to show you what is real, and together work it out! Don't allow these unprocessed feelings to marinate just below the surface, waiting for one "fool" to cut you off in traffic or one loudmouth to ignite a reaction even they didn't deserve.

DAY 5

Scripture Focus

1 Samuel 26–27:1

It seems like the madness never stopped for David. Have you ever known someone or even been someone who seems to just experience one painful event after another? It makes you wonder, *When is enough, Lord?*

Honestly, I don't have the answer for that. I have felt like that person on several occasions, wondering if God truly cares and questioning what He is trying to teach me. *How will all of this work together for my good? When will the light at the end of the tunnel come?* Then one day you realize that this life *is* the tunnel. You realize that life is more about preparation than outcome.

As we return to our story, we will see that once again, David has been betrayed and Saul is on his way for another round of hide-and-seek.

Read 1 Samuel 26:1-4. What is happening?

Basically, the army of Saul had shown up in the area, and David had sent out a spy to see if Saul himself was with them.

Now describe in your own words what happens in 1 Samuel 26:5-12. Write it out as if you are telling the story to middle schoolers. Put yourself in the story. Use all of your senses to describe the scene.

Saul was sleeping in a highly protected area. He was literally in the middle of three thousand soldiers, and his number one bodyguard was sleeping right next to him. He felt completely safe. But was he? David and Abishai snuck quietly into the middle of Saul's camp unnoticed. Don't forget who David was. He was one of the greatest leaders in Saul's army, not to mention Saul's own armor-bearer. David knew their ways, and he knew what he was doing.

There David and Abishai were, staring down at the sleeping madman who had been chasing them all over the known world. Once again Abishai wanted to run him through with Saul's own spear. He even promised David that he would make it quick and painless. I can just imagine David saying, "Are you kidding, Abishai? How in the world would you do that and get out of here alive? Plus, this is an old conversation. He is God's anointed."

Extra Insight

During this time in ancient Israel, armies used three categories of weapons. Daggers and swords were used for hand-to-hand combat, and javelins and some spears were thrown as a mid-range weapon. Long-range weapons included slings and bows and arrows.[20]

I can't imagine all the thoughts that ran through David's mind as he looked down on Saul. The man he once knew. The man Saul had become. This man who had taken everything from him—and for what? If we were watching this play out in a movie, we probably would be freaking out as David stared down at Saul. I would be screaming for him to hurry and get away. Once again, he refused to touch God's anointed but instead took some things to prove he was there.

Why did David refuse to lay a hand on Saul? (vv. 9-10)

What items did David take? (vv. 11-12)

David refused to give in to violence in order to free himself of pain. By doing so, we see that David was willing to sit in the pain and wait for God to move. To be honest, living with the pain is so hard for me. When I am sad and heartbroken, I honestly want to do anything to make it stop.

What about you? Have you ever made a choice you regret because you just wanted to stop the pain? Have you ever forfeited growth for comfort? Has there been a time in your life when you wish you would have sat a little longer in the pain and discomfort before making a decision? Has there been a time when sitting in the pain was your only choice? Journal below.

Read 1 Samuel 26:13-16, and rewrite David's words to Abner (the commander of Saul's army) in your own words.

Here's my version: "Abner, you think you are a true and loyal bodyguard for the king? You proclaim to be his loyal subject and protector, while I am portrayed as an enemy. Who is actually the loyal subject here? Me or you? I literally snuck into your encampment and took your master's spear while you slept next to him. I easily could have killed him on the spot. If anyone deserves death, it is you for failing to do your job to protect the king of Israel. I have had every chance to kill him and yet I have shown him great respect. What about you?" Can't you just hear the frustration in David's voice?

Now read 1 Samuel 26:17-25. Who interrupted David's speech, and what did he ask?

What did David then ask Saul?

I can't help but wonder if Saul's intention was to keep David talking while he sent a group of men to track his voice and kill him—kind of like keeping the bad guy on the phone long enough to track his whereabouts. Yet David must have thought the risk was worth it. He asked Saul, "What have I done?" He was probably trying to get Saul to think about the situation. How did it get this far? What had David actually done? What was his crime?

David told Saul that no matter what had brought him to this moment, he could stop. It was not too late. This whole thing could be fixed. He was trying to make Saul really think about what he was doing and to give him a way out. David basically said, "If this evil spirit from the Lord is still vexing you, please seek the Lord with sacrifice. Oh, my king, get right. Repent. Yet if it is other people's opinions, please, my king, look at the facts."

Sometimes we may think we have gone too far to turn back. We won't risk humiliation to find restoration. We won't risk being wrong to find unity. We won't risk swallowing our pride to find help. We believe too much damage

It is never too late to do the right thing.

has been done. But that is not true! It is never too late to do the right thing. David was attempting to show Saul that there was still time, essentially saying, "Please be reasonable."

I can sense David's desperation as he clung to the hope that *this time* the power of love and faithfulness would break through and Saul would see the damage he was causing, and I'm reminded of the words of Proverbs 3:3 (NIV), "Let love and faithfulness never leave you; / bind them around your neck, / write them on the tablet of your heart."

I can imagine David pleading, "You know I am innocent, yet you are pushing my men and me out of God's land, away from the people and presence of God. You are abandoning us to the influences of other gods. This has become so much bigger than you and me. Please, my king, see what you are doing to your family and your nation. Please see what you are doing to me!"

How did Saul respond in 1 Samuel 26:21?

18-20My dear children, let's not just talk about love; let's practice real love. This is the only way we'll know we're living truly, living in God's reality. It's also the way to shut down debilitating self-criticism, even when there is something to it. For God is greater than our worried hearts and knows more about us than we do ourselves.

(1 John 3:18-20 MSG)

Read 1 John 3:18-20 in the margin. How would you describe the difference between talking about love and practicing love?

Talk is cheap. If only Saul would have truly surrendered and trusted God—let go of control, let go of power and image, let go of self-criticism, own his failures, accept forgiveness, and practice, or walk, in God's love.

Although David desired the words of Saul to be true, he probably knew they weren't.

According to 1 Samuel 26:22, what did David allow Saul to do?

David used this act of releasing Saul's spear as a witness to his words. Every time Saul looked at his spear, David wanted Saul to remember that David could have used it to kill him but did not. He wanted Saul to remember that no matter if he was surrounded by three thousand men and had his weapon right by his side, God was actually in control. God had placed Saul into David's hands, and out of respect for God's anointed, David did not kill him. David was reminding Saul that just as he saved and protected the king, God would do the same for David (v. 24). David may not have had the full army of Israel at his disposal, but he had the protection of Yahweh.

We also need to remember that we can do everything in our power to build our high towers to protect ourselves from the floodwaters of trouble, but ultimately God is in control. No matter what precautions we take to ward off or protect ourselves from natural disasters, viruses, or the violent acts of men, our lives and our security lie ultimately in the hands of God.

Look again at verse 25 and read between the lines. What was Saul essentially saying here?

Saul surely knew in his heart that David would be the next king. He proclaimed, "You shall surely triumph." Yet, as we will see once again, every time he seemed to accept it, fear came in and stirred the waters.

When was the last time you made a decision because it was the right thing to do? How hard was it to stick to what you had decided when all of the fear and heartache came flooding in? Did you stick to it? Describe the situation below.

It seems that, for a moment, Saul allowed the scales of fear to fall from his eyes, acknowledging that what David was saying was right. It reads like a brief moment of surrender. Yet, once the moment passed and the "what ifs" returned, all previous clarity was clouded by his present fear.

Such anxiety sends us running back to our old comforts. Fear is the fuel that ignites the fires of control. For Saul, it seems that this was making David

Fear is the fuel that ignites the fires of control.

the object of his envy, jealousy, and rage. Perhaps if he could stay focused on chasing David, he would not have to deal with the true issues within himself.

David, likely anticipating that another storm would come, decided he had to make some changes.

Read 1 Samuel 27:1. What did David decide to do and why?

Today's lesson may seem like just another story of paranoid Saul chasing down David, causing all kinds of pain yet proving unsuccessful. This story line is kind of getting old. But isn't that the point? I think this is what is happening in 1 Samuel 27:1. Once again David had pleaded with Saul to change his ways, and once again there was talk but no change. David was getting sick of his own story line! He was exhausted and weary. I believe a little hopelessness was setting in, too. He was buying the lie that this was the narrative of his life and nothing was ever going to change it.

Have you ever lived in the space of "whatever, I don't care anymore"? I have too, my friend. But even there, God is with us.

Prayer Prompt

If you find yourself in the space where every response you have to life is "whatever," resist this dark cloud of apathy. Dig deep and find your grit. It is there! Pour out your complaints to God. Pour out your fears. Pour out your doubts. Ask Him to remind you of His great love for you and renew your faith! Whatever you do, stay in the land of faithfulness.

When you find yourself in the dark cave of loss, it can be very hard not

to _____ God.

Jesus is acquainted with all of our _____. He knows what it feels like to be fully

_____.

_____ can separate us from the love of God!

Some things just can't be fully grasped; we must leave it to _____.

Pain is a part of the _____. Drop any unnecessary _____

and persevere through the pain.

More people are drawn to your _____ than your fake perfection.

Scriptures: 1 Samuel 22; Psalm 142:4; Matthew 27:46; Romans 8:35, 38-39;
        Acts 2:22-23; Jeremiah 29:11; Romans 8:18; Hebrews 12:1

Week 6

God Really Is in Control

Coming Full Circle to True Belief and Surrender

1 Samuel 27–31

DAY 1

We ended last week with David contemplating a great escape. *The Message* Bible expresses David's thoughts this way: "Sooner or later, Saul's going to get me. The best thing I can do is escape to Philistine country. Saul will count me a lost cause and quit hunting me down in every nook and cranny of Israel. I'll be out of his reach for good" (1 Samuel 27:1 MSG).

Do you recognize the hopelessness that seems to have set in for David? When we're hopeless, we don't see any way that things can improve. David may have been falling into thinking, "This is just the way it is. These are the cards I have been dealt, and there is nothing I can do to change it." I call that kind of thinking a pity party. Though I'm speculating, I wouldn't blame David if he felt that way. When you've experienced as much pain as David had, it would be hard not to have a little self-pity.

It seems clear that David was tired of the battle. He was tired of the anxiety. He was tired of the stress and sorrow. He was tired of doing everything he could to fix the problem with nothing seeming to change. He wanted some comfort, some normalcy, some control. Even if he had to settle for a much smaller kingdom.

Have you ever come to a place in your life where you are willing to settle? After years of battling, you are convinced that the things you once dreamed of either don't exist or they don't exist for *you*. You've tried to be obedient and strong, but nothing ever seems to work out. You concede that you are destined to repeat the same old patterns. So you push those dreams aside and move to the land of "settle" because you need to be seen, to be heard, and to belong.

When you have lost control, what dreams have you given up and what "lands" have you settled in? Write about it briefly below.

My friend, you aren't alone. Let's hit pause on David's story briefly and consider a woman in Scripture who felt the need to settle. Her name is Leah.

Read Genesis 29. In what way did Leah have to settle, and why?

After running for his life from his older brother, Esau, Jacob ended up at the well of Laban. When Jacob saw Laban's younger daughter, Rachel, who the Bible says was beautiful, he fell in love. He promised to work seven years for Rachel's hand in marriage. Yet when the wedding night came, Laban switched his older daughter, Leah, for the younger. Probably with a little help from alcohol, Jacob consummated his marriage but was completely unaware he was with the wrong woman. You can imagine Jacob's response when he saw Leah in the morning. He ran out of his tent ready to remove the head of his uncle.

At the end of the day, Jacob wound up with two wives—which is never a good plan, especially when one is loved and the other is not.

Allow yourself to sit in the shoes of Leah for just a minute. Your whole life you have taken a backseat in every way to your younger, more beautiful sister. Now your father, in an attempt to get rid of you, tricks a man into marrying you—a man who does not love you but instead loves your younger sister. Express how you would feel.

I cannot imagine the pain Leah felt when she saw the look on Jacob's face as he discovered at morning's light that he had married the wrong woman. How excruciating and humiliating. Who knows what kinds of things came out of Jacob's mouth? Yet the story goes on to tell us that it was Leah who began to have children. And it is in the names of her children that we are given a front-row seat to her pain.

Leah's first son had the name Reuben, which means "behold a son,"[1] or as *The Message* **Bible translates it, "Look-It's-a-Boy!" What does Genesis 29:32 tell us about Leah's true desire?**

Leah's second son was named Simeon, which means "he has heard."[2] Fill in the blank according to verse 33:

"Because the LORD *has _____ that I am hated, he has given me this son also."*

Leah conceived yet again and gave birth to Levi, which means "joined, attached."[3] Write verse 34 below.

What was happening here? What cycle of pain was Leah experiencing? She was doing what we all do when we are in pain. First we want someone to see us. I can imagine what Leah might have been thinking when she named her first son Reuben: "Look at me. See who I am. Look what I have done. I have given you a son. Look! Look! Look! Now am I enough?"

Then, with the birth of Simeon, she wanted to be heard. I wonder if she might have thought something like this: "I am not loved. Please hear me. Please listen to me. Please understand the situation I am in." Yet perhaps secretly she believed that no one truly understood her pain.

Then, just when she might have thought her pain had silenced all hope, she named her third son Levi—"joined, attached." Maybe with this boy, Jacob would at least be attached to her. Leah wanted what every human being on the planet wants and needs: to be seen, to be heard, and to have connection. Yet in her pain and isolation, look what had happened.

Fill in the missing words below according to verses 32 and 34:

"Because the LORD **has looked upon my affliction; for now my husband will _____ me." (v. 32)**

"Now this time my husband will be _____ to me,

because I have borne him three sons." (v. 34)

What a person desires is unfailing love.
(Proverbs 19:22a NIV)

At first Leah wanted to be loved (v. 32). Every human being desires love (see Proverbs 19:22a in the margin). But it seems that Leah had been so worn down by her pain that she was willing to settle. Apparently she had given up on love and was willing to settle for attachment (Genesis 29:34). If not love, then at least some element of connection.

The beauty in this story is that Leah had a fourth son. She named him Judah, which means "praise."

What did Leah say in Genesis 29:35?

God sees *you*. You are enough. God hears you, and He understands what you are going through. You are not alone!

This pain in Leah's life brought her to the greatest discovery of life: God sees each of us. God sees *you*. You are enough. God hears you, and He understands what you are going through. You are not alone! You belong to Him.

Now let's get back to our story in 1 Samuel. Throughout David's pain, he had attempted to make Saul look at him (see 1 Samuel 24:11). To see the situation. To see the truth. To see that he was not a threat. David had also begged Saul to listen to his voice, to hear him, and to understand what Saul was doing to him (see 1 Samuel 26:17-19). Yet Saul never changed. He never stopped chasing David. David was weary of the fight. He was tired of running, so he chose to go to the land of the Philistines.

Wait a minute. Hadn't David been to Gath before? And if I am remembering correctly, it didn't work out too well.

Look back at 1 Samuel 21:10-15. What happened last time David ran to the land of the Philistines?

Going back to Gath was a risky move. Why do you think David was willing to take that risk?

Remember, the first time David fled Israel as a fugitive, very few people were aware of what was going on. Even the Israelite priests were unaware of the falling out between David and Saul. They wondered why David had shown up alone without his armor guard. Before Saul put them to death, the high priest adamantly proclaimed his innocence, stating, "Your servant has known nothing of all this" (1 Samuel 22:15). If the men of David's own land did not realize that he had been branded a traitor, it's safe to say the word had not made it to the Philistine territories.

The first time David showed up in Gath, he was seen as the hero of Israel and enemy of the Philistines. To put it in modern terms, David had essentially shown up in one of their towns alone, dressed in a black hoodie, armed, and attempting to stay under the radar. This scenario shouts "spy" all the way! When the men of Gath saw David, they knew something wasn't right and took him immediately to Achish. Do you remember how David ultimately escaped? Yep. He acted insane!

Despite the previous experience, David went back to the city of Gath.

Read 1 Samuel 27:2-4. Who was with David in Gath? (vv. 2-3)

What was Saul's response to the news of David's whereabouts?

This time, David was accompanied by six hundred men and their families, including David's wives, Ahinoam and Abigail. And this time, the whole world knew that David was an enemy of Israel. The Philistines had actually used this to their advantage. When Saul and his army had been out looking for David, the Philistines had used these opportunities to strike Israel. So, when David showed up requesting asylum, Achish gave it to him this time. And Saul gave up the hunt.

At first it seemed that David's crew would stay in Gath, but quickly David made a request. What did he request in verse 5?

It's safe to assume that David didn't actually want to live among the Philistines. He was not one of them, nor would he have desired that. What he desired was his own little kingdom—a separate place away from the stresses and dangers of Israel and Gath. He would be able to retreat to his own small kingdom, his safe place.

According to 1 Samuel 27:6-7, what territory did Achish give David?

How long did David live there?

Ziklag was approximately twenty-five miles southeast of Gath and not very far from Israelite cities. It was a pretty good middle ground between the two. Ziklag was also far enough away from Gath that Achish would be unaware of David's movements. We might think of it as moving far enough away from family that they wouldn't be all up in our business yet close enough to visit. David stayed there a year and four months.

Read 1 Samuel 27:8-12. Now that David had his territory, what did he do for his livelihood?

Why did he not leave anyone alive?

David used Ziklag as his base of operation and from there he conducted raids on the surrounding people groups, taking their "sheep, cattle, donkeys, camels, clothing—the works" (vv. 8-9 MSG). He didn't leave anyone alive because he used the loot to convince Achish that he was raiding his own people, the Israelites, and he could not afford to leave any witnesses to the contrary. Some of these "ites" may be less familiar to us, such as the Amalekites, but Scripture says that these were ancient inhabitants of the land; therefore, we can assume that they all would be in the category of the Canaanites, whom God had warned His people about intermixing with. In fact, as the Israelites were preparing to enter the Promised Land years before, God had instructed them not to make treaties or intermarry with the Canaanites so that the Israelites wouldn't be drawn into the natives' pagan worship. God told the Israelites to conquer these people (see Deuteronomy 7:1-5).

Because of this directive, some argue that David was obeying the law in his quest to conquer the land given to Israel by God. Yet, I can't help but wonder if it was more of a pragmatic choice than a spiritual one. Could David have been protecting his own little kingdom? Was David consulting God in these decisions?

Extra Insight

The Amalekites were nomadic descendants of Amalek, the child of Eliphaz and his concubine, Timna. Amalek's grandfather was Esau, the brother of patriarch Jacob. The Amalekites lived south of Israel in an area now known as the Negev Desert.[4]

Whatever his intention, his strategy worked. First Samuel 27 ends with this statement: "And Achish trusted David, thinking, 'He has made himself an utter stench to his people Israel; therefore he shall always be my servant'" (v. 12).

Isn't it amazing how screwed up everything gets when we take the reins? At this point Saul was convinced David was his enemy, but he wasn't; Achish was convinced that David was his ally, but he wasn't.

Everyone around us may appear comfortable and in control, but trust me, appearances can lie. God sees past appearances and knows the truth. Honestly, when it comes to our own lives, we know the truth, too—that is, if we are honestly willing to be self-aware. Most of the time, the problem is that we don't want to risk our comfort to truly *look inside* ourselves, because we might be compelled to act by what we see.

Friend, let's not play charades but choose to look, see, and act.

Prayer Prompt

Ask the Father to highlight for you any personal application regarding the contrast of appearance versus truth in your life. How will you respond to what He shows you?

DAY 2

As we study the last chapters of 1 Samuel, we have to be aware that they are not written in chronological order. That would be very difficult for the author to do considering many of the events were happening simultaneously. Therefore, for better understanding, I am going to do my best to maneuver us through this story. Just know that from here on out, we will not be traveling through the chapters in verse-by-verse order.

Scripture Focus

1 Samuel 28:1-2;
1 Samuel 29;
1 Samuel 30:1-6

Read 1 Samuel 28:1. Tensions between the Philistines and the Israelites had grown. What were the Philistines preparing to do?

Why do you think Achish would say, "Understand that you and your men are to go out with me in the army"?

During the past year, David had proven to Achish that he was completely loyal to him. Achish believed David had been raiding the Israelites and that

David's true allegiance was with him. Achish was convinced of David's hatred toward Israel, and especially Saul, for what they had done to him. Now this was Achish's opportunity to prove his loyalty to David. He saw this as an honor. He was saying to David, "I trust you so completely that I am taking you and your men into battle against Israel as part of my own army."

Let me tell you something: David was a really good actor! Not only could he play the role of an insane person, but he also could pull off trusted ally pretty dang well, too. David was amazing at painting whatever image of himself he needed to survive. One probably gets really good at this when running for one's life.

Fear causes us to protect our vulnerable selves.

What about you? Are you good at presenting whatever image you need in order to survive or achieve? Listen, I don't blame anyone for that. I am the best at it! Fear causes us to protect our vulnerable selves. From childhood, we learn how to protect ourselves in whatever environment we grow up in. We read our environment and then we learn to adjust and maneuver for acceptance and love.

When was the last time you sat down in a quiet, safe place and truly asked yourself questions such as these: *Who am I, really? How did I get here? And is "here" where I want to be? Do people truly know the real me?*

Take a moment now to reflect on these questions:

Do others know the real me? Why or why not?

Do *I* know the real me, or do I just see myself through other people's filters? Explain.

I have to say: The *real* you is the best version!
As for David, he felt he still had to play a role.

Read 1 Samuel 28:2. What do you think David meant when he said, "Very well, you shall know what your servant can do"? Write your interpretation below.

Based on Achish's response, what did he believe David's words meant?

David's response is hard to interpret, especially without seeing his body language or hearing his inflection.

Say David's words (below) out loud twice. The first time, say them with sincerity. The second time, say them with a little bit of a sinister edge.

"Very well, you shall know what your servant can do."

Do you still agree with the interpretation you wrote above, or have you changed your mind? Explain.

Either way, it had been decided: David and his men were joining with the Philistines to battle against the Israelites.

Read 1 Samuel 29:1-3. What is the conflict in these verses?

All the regimens from the five main Philistine cities along the Mediterranean Sea gathered together at Aphek. Once the army was fully assembled, they would march together to the Jezreel valley. According to verse 2, most of the Philistine warlords had already gathered with their regimens and divisions at Aphek when Achish finally showed up. When the other Philistine warlords realized that some Israelites were among Achish's troops, they objected.

Write Achish's response to their question, found in verse 3, in your own words.

Extra Insight

Aphek was an ancient town situated by the Mediterranean coastal plain and the base of the Judean hills. It was a post on the Via Maris, the trading route between Egypt and Mesopotamia. King Herod the Great changed the name of the town to Anipatris as a tribute to his father, who bore that name. An earthquake destroyed the city in 363 AD.[5]

What would you have said to convince the Philistine warlords of David's loyalty?

Achish had bought David's deception hook, line, and sinker, but the other warlords—not so much. They had not had the privilege of watching David work, hearing his stories, or sharing his loot. They had not experienced this "new" David, and they were not convinced.

According to verses 4-5, what did the other warlords decide about David?

Were they actually wrong to have fear? Had the Philistines been burned before with this kind of situation? Read 1 Samuel 14:16-23, and describe what happened in that battle below.

How does the saying go? *Fool me once, shame on you. Fool me twice, shame on me!* These warlords remembered that previous war begun by Jonathan's bravery. In that battle, as soon as the Israelites started to gain momentum, the Israelites who had previously deserted to the Philistine side switched and began fighting once again for Israel. This caused so much confusion that the Philistines lost the battle. In such a situation, you wouldn't know whom to fight.

These commanders remembered that battle and would not repeat the same mistake again. Hey, you've got to give it to them. How many times would they fall for the same trap?

Have you ever fallen for the same trap twice? It might be good just to write it out and acknowledge it below.

Now read 1 Samuel 29:6-11. What attributes did Achish give David in verses 6 and 9?

Was David's final appeal successful? Explain.

Even after pressing Achish, this time David's finesse and theatrics did not work. David and his men were sent home. By the way, why do you think David wanted to go to battle with the Philistines so badly—or did he? Was this to be his crowning maneuver, his final attempt to once again become the hero of Israel? Or could this have been God getting him out of one of the most impossible situations he had ever been in?

I cannot imagine how David felt on his way home. He was either extremely frustrated that a long-laid plan had fallen through or unbelievably relieved that he had not been placed in a situation to fight against his own people.

Read 1 Samuel 30:1-3. After turning around and marching three more days back to Ziklag, what did David and his men discover?

David may have dodged a bullet with the Philistines, but when he arrived back home and saw what the Amalekites had done to Ziklag, I'm sure he felt like he had taken one in the gut. The Amalekites had raided Ziklag, burned it to the ground, and taken their families.

Write 1 Samuel 30:4 below.

Already exhausted and defeated, this blow was devastating. When these men realized what had happened in their absence, they burst into wailing. They literally wept and wept until they had no more tears. While they were out proving appearances, securing the safety of their families from the Philistines, another enemy had attacked. This was too much for them to bear.

Read 1 Samuel 30:5-6. How did the people react to David, their leader?

What did David do, according to verse 6?

Not only did David share in the people's grief, having lost his own two wives, but he also became the source of their grief. They blamed David for what had happened. I can imagine them saying something like this: "This is all your fault, David. We have been loyal to you from the beginning. We came to you as a bunch of misfits, and you turned us into an army. We have followed you faithfully wherever you have led us—into the deserts and the caves. We have never questioned your leadership, even when we had Saul in our grasp twice and you refused to kill him. We have even followed you into enemy territory. And now our families have paid the price. Where is this God you so trust? Where is this kingdom he has given you? Where is peace? We no longer care. All is lost!"

I remember one season in life when I was so focused on helping my son Zach with some issues he was having at college that I missed some obvious signs of danger in my daughter Hillary's life. I should have seen it, but I didn't. While I was out focusing on how to handle one battle, another unexpected battle hit, and it definitely left behind ashes.

Have you ever felt attacked on multiple sides? How did you react?

> **God, give me eyes to see what You want me to see and ears to hear what You want me to hear.**

Listen, we can't be everywhere all the time. We can't see everything all the time. We can only do so much! What I have learned to pray lately is, "God, give me eyes to see what You want me to see and ears to hear what You want me to hear." God was not unaware of what was going on in Ziklag, and He got David and his men back home, dare I say just in time.

Read 1 Samuel 30:17-20. What happened?

Oh, the beauty God can bring out of ashes!

When everything we do seems to just make matters worse and those closest to us have lost hope—or worse, they blame us for their problems—we can look to David's example. There is such beauty in these words: "But David strengthened himself in the LORD his God" (v. 6). Only then did David have the strength and wisdom to act. Only then could God direct him in what to do next.

We can have the best intentions. We can make the best decisions we can based on the information we have. We can be convinced in our hearts that we are on the right path doing God's will, yet we can still end up in a place of defeat. At first we grieve, and then we may blame others or ourselves. We analyze every step that got us to this place. We play the *shoulda, woulda, coulda* game. But eventually we must come to a place of being alone with God, shutting down all the other voices in our lives, and asking Him, "Where do I go from here?"

I don't know about you, but I relate to these words of the apostle Paul: "I'm not saying that I have this all together, that I have it made. But I am well on my way, reaching out for Christ, who has so wondrously reached out for me. Friends, don't get me wrong: By no means do I count myself an expert in all of this, but I've got my eye on the goal, where God is beckoning us onward—to Jesus. I'm off and running, and I'm not turning back" (Philippians 3:12-14 MSG).

We may not have it all together. David certainly didn't. But when we lose control, we can follow his example and turn our eyes to God, for He is our greatest hope. Whatever detours we have taken, Jesus is the gate back to the right path.

Prayer Prompt

If today you need to play the shoulda, woulda, coulda game for a while, go ahead. Spend as much time there as you need, but don't stay there. Get all of the shame, blame, and regret out, and then strengthen yourself in the Lord. Say to Him, "Okay, where do I go from here?"

DAY 3

Yesterday in our study we considered the devastation at Ziklag, including the capture of David's wives and all the women and children of his people. David and his men were in deep despair, and then David encouraged himself in the Lord. For some reason, I want to start today's lesson with, "Meanwhile, back on the home front . . ." in reference to Saul. It's a little cheesy, I know, but remember these events are happening simultaneously.

Scripture Focus

1 Samuel 28

Read 1 Samuel 28:3. What two things does this verse tell us?

This verse seems so random when we first encounter it. Yet, as we continue to read the chapter, we will realize that the author is giving us some important background information. First, he is reminding us that Samuel was dead; and second, under Samuel's influence, Saul had previously cleared out all the mediums and spiritists from the land.

Read Leviticus 19:31 and 20:6 in the margin. What insights do these verses give us regarding why Saul expelled the mediums and spiritists?

Now read 1 Samuel 28:4-6. What was happening, and what prompted Saul to seek a medium?

At this point in our story, both armies had now arrived at the battlefield, the valley of Jezreel. The Israelites had assembled on Mount Gilboa, and the Philistines at Shunem. Notice in 1 Samuel 28:5 it says that when Saul saw the army of the Philistines, he was afraid. *The Message* puts it like this: "When Saul *saw* the Philistine troops, he shook in his boots, scared to death" (emphasis added). Saul was continuing to live by sight and not by faith.

Living by sight is one of the earliest tactics of the enemy of our souls. Oh, the gateway of the eye. "When the woman *saw* that the tree was good for food, and that it was a *delight to the eyes*, and that the tree was to be desired to make one wise, she took of its fruit…" (Genesis 3:6, emphasis added). How often does what we see make us question the goodness and faithfulness of our God?

When has what you *saw* made you question God's goodness or faithfulness?

Speaking of "seeing," are you seeing Saul's pattern? Let's do a quick walk down memory lane.

After reading each verse, write what it says Saul feared.

1. 1 Samuel 15:24   _____

2. 1 Samuel 17:11   _____

3. 1 Samuel 18:12   _____

Answers: 1. People 2. Goliath 3. David 4. Jonathan 5. Philistines

4. 1 Samuel 22:8   _____

5. 1 Samuel 28:5   _____

According to Proverbs 9:10 in the margin, what healthy fear is missing from this list?

The fear of the LORD is the beginning of wisdom, and the knowledge of the Holy One is insight. (Proverbs 9:10)

The fear of the Lord is not the same as the kind of fear that Saul experienced in these other situations. The former is reverence that leads to wisdom, while the latter is terror that consumes and destroys. Wisdom is all about perspective. According to Proverbs 9:10, being able to make wise decisions—to mentally separate things out—begins with our recognition and acknowledgment of the Holy One. It is about our perspective. He is God, and we are not.

Let's apply this to Saul. Why was he filled with terror? Because he had lost proper perspective. Wisdom begins with the reverence of God. Saul refused to relinquish control to God. He had confused his earthly reign for divine sovereignty, and yet somewhere deep down he knew he had bought into a lie. He knew he had no real power. Yet, it seems like the more he realized this, the more he strove for control. I find myself wanting to scream, "Saul, just let go! Let the cup spill. See what the Lord will do. Trust that He is good!"

An article I read on fear versus power says this: "Underlying the quest for power is fear, and the desire for power is to eliminate fear. The more fearful a person is, the more control over their environment they believe they need to feel safe."[6] How ironic. Often leaders use fear to bolster their power, yet it is their own fear that feeds their need for such power.

Reread 1 Samuel 28:6. Does this verse rub you the wrong way? Why or why not?

You may be crying out, "But Mary Shannon, Saul was seeking the Lord, and the Lord was not speaking!" If that's you, I feel your pain. But let me ask you, had God spoken to Saul before? And did he listen?

I believe that sometimes God remains silent because He has already told us what we need to hear. Why would God give us new information when we won't obey or act on the information He has already given us? On the outside, Saul seemed to be seeking God, yet on the inside Saul needed to repent.

Don't forget all that Saul had done to hinder the lines of communication between himself and God. In the Old Testament, God typically communicated in one of three ways: personal revelation, prophets or priests, and the Urim and Thummin. According to 1 Samuel 28:6, we know that God did not choose to speak to Saul at that time through personal revelation. We also know God did not speak through a prophet. I can think of a pretty good reason for that! Samuel was dead, and certainly the other prophets of the day knew that Saul's kingdom was no longer recognized before the Lord. If Saul wouldn't obey the words of Samuel, then why would the words of any other prophet make any difference? This brings us to the final mode of communication.

The priests were the mediators between God and people, and they had been given an amazing tool to use when asking God for yes or no answers: the Urim and the Thummin, which we read about earlier in our study (page 54). But remember, Saul ordered the deaths of all the priests of Nob and their families (1 Samuel 22:6-23). The only survivor was Abiathar, and Scripture tells us that he escaped to David with the ephod. So guess who had the dice? Yep, David. And while Saul was inquiring about the Philistines, David was inquiring about rescuing his family from the Amalekites.

Yet none of this would stop Saul. He was determined to find the answer he wanted. Do you get the idea that Saul was just going to keep looking until he found someone who would tell him what he wanted to hear? When all we want are yes men, we are in real trouble. I pray often that God continues to give me friends who will tell me what I need to hear and not what I want to hear.

Read 1 Samuel 28:7-10. Why was it necessary for Saul to put on a disguise?

Isn't it interesting that although Saul, under the influence of Samuel, had rid the land of all mediums, his own men did not seem too hard pressed to find one when he needed one? This might suggest to us a spiritual vacuum created by the death of Samuel. Saul might have cleaned house, but somehow this evil had crept back in (see also Luke 11:24-26).

En-dor was quite a little trip for Saul. It was a six-mile journey, and it was located two miles northeast of the Philistine camp. Not only did Saul need a disguise to get past the Philistines, but he also needed one for the destination. Years before, he himself had been the one to run all the mediums and spiritists out of the land, and he was unlikely to be welcomed into this woman's home if she knew who Saul was (1 Samuel 28:9). What happened next is very concerning.

Write verse 10 in your own words below to express what you think Saul was really saying here.

Saul had become so arrogant that he thought he could promise this woman no repercussions from God as long as she did what he wanted. In other words, he was putting his own desires above God's commands. Wow, that sounds horrible, doesn't it? Yet, isn't that what we call justification—when we believe we must put our own needs above God's desires? Well, when I put it like that, I am *summa cum laude* in the school of justification.

When was the last time you chose to justify your actions? A time when you bought the lie that some deep desire or fear was more important than following God? You might say to yourself, *Surely God understands*. He does! He completely understands. He knows why you did it and He knows how you feel, but He also knows that His commands are the words of life. He is literally leading us to paths of life and freedom. That is why Jesus came—so that we might have life and freedom.

Justification is the self-deception that our attempts to meet our own wants or calm our own fears will bring us contentment or peace. Yet it never works out that way. It may satisfy for a moment, but the aftertaste can be a beast!

Read 1 Samuel 28:11-20 and answer the following:

Whom did Saul want the medium to bring up? (v. 11)

What did Saul ask of him? (v. 15)

What message did Samuel give? (vv. 17-19)

What was Saul's response? (v. 20)

Some scholars speculate whether this was an actual appearance of Samuel. Allow me to share five reasons one might consider:

1. The medium was shocked at his appearance. (This makes me laugh every time.)
2. Saul seemed to recognize him based on his description. (Did Saul ask the witch if the hem of Samuel's robe was ripped?)
3. The narrator of this passage seems to credit this person as Samuel.
4. The conversation between Saul and Samuel seems very familiar.
5. The message of Samuel did not change.[8]

What added information was Saul given in verse 19? What was his response to this information?

All of this was finally too much for Saul to bear!

The insecurities

The successes   The failures

The judgments   The image problem

The envy

The fear

The jealousy   The rage

The paranoia

The chase

The wars

Death

This downward spiral sent Saul to the floor. Exhausted from his attempt to control, he collapsed!

Read 1 Samuel 28:21-25. What did the woman do to strengthen Saul?

We will never know the motive behind the woman's generosity, but I am sure it is never a good thing when a king passes out on your floor. And it's probably a good idea to do everything you can to get him to leave on good terms. She picked him up and gave him a good pep talk, saying something like this: "Saul, you need to pull yourself together, man. I have done everything that you have asked. Now eat something so you will be strong enough to go. You have an army waiting for you!" I'm sure she had no desire for the war to come to her home! Saul refused. He literally didn't care. It took the added speeches of his servants to convince him to eat, but eventually he did. Once strengthened, he made his way back to Mount Gilboa.

We are not given any more information into the psyche of Saul. At this point, he seems resolved to fight, knowing he would not live to see another day. I cannot help but hear the ringing of Proverbs 14:12:

> There is a way that seems right to a man,
> but its end is the way to death.

Saul finally understood that all of his fighting for control was to no end. He was not in control. God was. Either we can fight God, leading to our own peril and a whole lot of pain for others, or we can surrender and receive life. The love of God cries out for us to trust Him, die to our egos (our desire for control), and allow our inner child to jump into the loving arms of the Father.

Are you ready to stop fighting, surrender, and jump into the Father's arms?

Prayer Prompt

Meditate on the following verse:

For it is written,

> "As I live, says the Lord, every knee shall bow to me,
> and every tongue shall confess to God."
> (Romans 14:11)

Will you choose to voluntarily submit to your loving Father, or will you wait until you realize you have no other choice? He desires sons and daughters, not slaves.

Either we can fight God, leading to our own peril and a whole lot of pain for others, or we can surrender and receive life.

DAY 4

Today we come to the battle between the Israelites and the Philistines on Mount Gilboa. The narrator spares us the gory details regarding the battle and instead skips to the heart of Israel's predicament: the Philistines were winning the war. In fact, they had proven to be so dominant that the Israelites were in full retreat. *The Message* says that the men of Israel were "falling left and right" before the Philistine army (v. 1)! But victory was not enough for the Philistines. They wanted total annihilation. They were determined to ride this momentum until Saul's head was on a platter.

Read 1 Samuel 31:1-6 and answer the following:

How was Saul badly wounded? (v. 3)

What did Saul ask of his armor-bearer, and what did the armor-bearer do? (v. 4)

How did Saul respond? (v. 4)

When the archers finally got Saul within range, they released their arrows. We have no idea how many of them found their target, but we know some did—enough to drop the king of Israel.

Teetering somewhere between life and death, Saul asked his armor-bearer to finish the job. He refused. Therefore, Saul fell on his own sword. Some suggest this was suicide, an act of desperation or exasperation. I would argue, however, that Saul did not give up but fought valiantly until the bitter end. I believe we find his true motivation in verse 4.

Fill in the blank below according to verse 4:

Then Saul said to his armor-bearer, "Draw your sword, and thrust me

through with it, lest these uncircumcised come and thrust me through,

and _____ *me."*

Saul knew his injuries were fatal, and he also knew what the Philistines would do to him if they found him with any breath remaining in his lungs. They would make sport with him in an attempt to humiliate him, the nation of Israel, and their God. I believe, therefore, that he took his own life as an act of honor—his final act as king. He chose to die with honor.

I wonder if this same stubbornness or pride that proved brave on the battlefield kept Saul from bowing his knee before God? I wish he had been as determined to live with honor as he was to die with it. If only he had been willing to die to self! Not the person God created him to be, but the false self he had become in an attempt to please the world and maintain control. I wish that self—Saul's ego—had fallen on a sword!

Read Proverbs 18:12 in the margin, and complete the following:

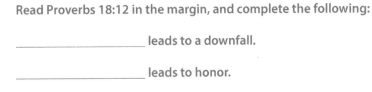

_____ leads to a downfall.

_____ leads to honor.

Before a downfall the heart is haughty, but humility comes before honor.
(Proverbs 18:12 NIV)

Haughtiness versus humility. Isn't it interesting that the serpent convinced Adam and Eve that if they ate the fruit from the forbidden tree, they would be like God? They were already like God, because they had been beautifully made in His image. Yet apparently that wasn't good enough. It seems they may have wanted to be *Godlike*, but that was impossible. So the deceptive serpent put them in a position to know good and evil, to be aware, and yet have no power to control the outcome. How miserable. He tempted them with knowledge and enslaved them in fear.

As we've seen throughout our study, fear is the root of all control issues. Fear of the unknown, fear of failure, fear of success, fear of change, fear of isolation, and fear of what others think. The more we fear, the more we try to control. The problem is that we do not have the power to control most things. We cannot control others and we cannot control outcomes. The only thing we can control is ourselves, and sometimes even that seems impossible. For me, often the more I try to control, the worse things get.

Fear is the root of all control issues.

Consider bending down and picking up a handful of sand. If you scoop the sand, keeping an open palm, you will actually be able to hold more sand. Yet if you squeeze your hand into a fist, trying to hold the sand tightly, what will happen? Yep, the sand will fall out between your fingers.

I often stop in stressful situations and ask myself, "Whose business am I meddling in? God's, my neighbor's, or mine?" The only one I can control is me. And according to Scripture, I need God for that one, too.

Now that we are near the end of our study, consider what insights or clarity you have received regarding your fears. Journal in response to the following questions: What are you afraid of? What or whom are you trying to control? Whose business are you in? What would happen if you stopped?

I can't help but wonder what would have happened in Israel if Saul would have humbled himself before the Lord and accepted the consequences of his actions. Would it have been painful and humbling? Yes. But what might the relationships in his home have been like as a result? What wars could have been avoided? What kind of mentor could he have been to David? How would his relationship with Samuel have changed?

Well, that is just speculation, and at this point in the saga there is nothing left to be done. Saul was dead, and the Israelites were defeated.

Read 1 Samuel 31:7-10. What details in these verses communicate how utterly defeated Israel was?

The defeat was so complete that the Israelites ran from their homes and the Philistines were moving right in! After the battle, the Philistines walked through the carnage, robbing the bodies of the Israelite soldiers and, of course, finishing off any who were still alive. The fact that the Philistines actually discovered the body of Saul also proves how utterly they defeated Israel. No soldier would have ever left the body of his dead king on the battlefield. Yet there was Saul.

The Philistines removed the heads of Saul and his sons to keep as trophies. They put his armor in the shrine of their fertility god, Ashtoreth. Then, after stripping their bodies, they nailed them to the walls of Beth-shan for the world to see. These were dark days in Israel.

I am so thankful that 1 Samuel does not end here.

Read 1 Samuel 31:11-13. Who heard what had happened to Saul and his sons and decided to risk their own lives to honor them?

Extra Insight

Ashtoreth, also known as Asherah, was the name of the chief female deity in ancient Canaan, Syria, and Phoenicia. Ashtoreth was the moon goddess and the counterpart to Baal, the sun god. It was also considered the goddess of love, and worship of it included ritual prostitution.[9]

What did they do?

Do you remember the people of Jabesh-gilead? In 1 Samuel 11, they were in a pickle. They were surrounded by the Ammonites, and king Nahash had refused their surrender unless they agreed to have their right eyes gouged out. Word had gotten back to Saul, who Scripture says was so filled with zeal that he assembled 300,000 Israelites for battle, ultimately freeing Jabesh from the Ammonites.

The people of Jabesh had not forgotten the faithfulness of Saul. Refusing to allow the bodies of Saul and his sons to be dishonored, they risked their own lives by traveling through Philistine-dominated territory at night and removed the bodies from the walls of Beth-shan. They brought them back to Israel and buried their bones according to tradition.

I cannot help but see the tenderness of God in this scene toward the family of Saul. When everyone else had deserted them, God remained faithful. I also see the power of lovingkindness. No matter what Saul had become, the people of Jabesh had not forgotten his kindness. Wow. It's amazing what an act of kindness can do. For all of Saul's failures, let's not forget his good deeds.

In order to properly put Saul and his reign to rest, it is necessary that we read a little of 2 Samuel. Having finally returned home after rescuing their families from the Amalekites, David and his men took a couple of days to recoup.

Read 2 Samuel 1:1-13 and answer the following:

Who showed up unannounced, and what was his outer appearance like? (v. 2) What did this kind of outer appearance typically signify (see Esther 4:3)?

What news did he share with David? Write all of the details below. (Notice that David did not just take him at his word but pressed him for more information.)

This young Amalekite showed up with every outer appearance of grief and told David about the defeat of Israel. He also informed him of the death of Saul and his son. (It's interesting to note that we see some similarities here to the story in 1 Samuel 21:7 and 22:9-23, which we explored in Week 4.)

Look back at 2 Samuel 1:13, and then read verse 14. Do you truly believe this Amalekite had sympathy for Saul? Or allegiance to David?

What do you think was his motive for bringing the crown and bands to David?

Remember, this was a time of war, and everyone was trying to find leverage for power and survival. I think this chump was just another enemy spy trying to infiltrate the ranks of Israel. But David was no dummy.

Read 2 Samuel 1:15-16. What action did David take, and why?

David recognized the spy's tactic and had the messenger executed. (He wouldn't ignore his instincts this time!)

Oh, sister! We too have an enemy, and he is a pro at the outward disguise! He loves to sit back and wait for painful events to happen in our lives because they create the perfect environment for him to plant a lie. Listen, we all experience those devastating events when someone or something dies. When our optimism dies. When our belief in God dies. When our innocence dies. When we learn to play a role for the first time. These events often begin early in our childhood, and we may not even be aware of how they impact us today. But somewhere along the way, our enemy crept in and deposited lies in our hearts and minds.

God is calling us to allow Him to show us our hidden places. Trust me, I know it is scary because your pain has likely been buried for a long time. That buried place is dark, and it probably stinks and is embarrassing. But we have to trust God in that place. To allow Him to heal us and replace whatever lie is hidden there with His truth.

Fear is what grows out of a lie. As we've seen throughout our study, digging down through the layers of our fears helps us determine the lies beneath.

I don't know about you, but I plan on "eliminating" any "spy" who tries to sabotage God's truth in my life! I have spent a lot of time digging up past pain to reveal any planted lies that produced fear. Therefore, today I commit to authenticity. When painful events come, and they will, I am determined to feel them and wrestle with any thoughts that accompany them. Truth be told, I am in a wrestling period now after enduring the greatest loss I have ever experienced. I hope you'll join me in this commitment to authenticity.

Prayer Prompt

If you are experiencing a time of grief or loss, ask God to protect you and to guard your thoughts. Whatever your thoughts are, friend, bring them to God. He can take it. Just ask Mary (John 11:32). He will weep with you and lead you down the road to healing. I'm counting on it!

DAY 5

As we say farewell to Saul, perhaps a parable of Jesus can help us to understand him better. It is called the parable of the lost son, but actually it is the story of two lost sons.

Scripture Focus

2 Samuel 1:17-27

Read the parable found in Luke 15:11-32, and describe below how each son was "lost."

The younger son:

The older son:

Both sons were alienated from their father. Both sons had to be invited into the party. The interesting thing is that the son who outwardly disrespected his father by demanding his inheritance and squandering it on wild living ultimately entered the celebration. He was shocked by the extravagant love and grace of his father. He was undeniably aware he didn't deserve it. What was lost was now found. Let the festivities begin!

Yet the story ends with the elder brother still standing outside, contemplating the father's invitation. The question we are left with is this: will this son see his need for the same extravagant love and grace?

In verse 29, when the elder brother says, "All these years I've been slaving for you" (NIV), he lets his underlying attitude and motives slip out. This was more than just a commitment to his duty. The word *slave* suggests being forced or pushed rather than drawn or attracted. As Tim Keller writes in his book *The Prodigal God*, "A slave works out of fear—fear of consequences imposed by force."[11] Elder brothers like the one in the parable live good lives out of fear, not out of joy or love.

There is no fear in love, but perfect love casts out fear. For fear has to do with punishment, and whoever fears has not been perfected in love.

(1 John 4:18)

No wonder he became so angry when his younger brother came back and his father threw him a party. How could this be? His younger brother was so disrespectful and so selfish! How could their father still love him? Then comes the real question in verse 29: *Why doesn't our father love me this much? He has never thrown me a party like that!* The elder brother had behaved well because he believed that's what it took to earn his father's love. He had done everything right. What more could the father have wanted from him?

Read 1 John 4:18 in the margin. Circle what casts out fear.

How can a love that is earned cast out fear? It can't.

Tim Keller identifies four signs that reveal whether we are suffering from this "elder brother" mentality:

Every time something goes wrong in your life or a prayer goes unanswered, you wonder if it's because you aren't living right in this or that area. Another sign is that criticism from others doesn't just hurt your feelings, it devastates you. This is because your sense of God's love is abstract and has little real power in your life, and you need the approval of others to bolster your sense of value. You will also feel irresolvable guilt.... But perhaps the clearest symptom of this lack of assurance is a dry prayer life.[12]

Wondering if we're not living right, being devastated by criticism, feeling irresolvable guilt, and having a dry prayer life—can we see these signs in our lives? Can we see them in Saul's life?

How do you see the signs of "elder brother" mentality in Saul's life? Spend some time thinking through the events of his life, recognizing these signs and describing them below.

I could cry over the amount of time I have attempted to control and manipulate God into loving me when He had already freely given His love.

The father of the two sons proclaimed to the eldest, "Everything I have is yours" (NIV)! If only the elder brother could have recognized that his good works weren't the solution. They only masked the underlying problem: pride. His prideful goodness was just as offensive as his younger brother's rebellious revelry; it was just harder for him to see because he had hidden it behind obedience. At the end of the story, we are left wondering if he accepted that revelation and entered the party of the father's love.

Which of these signs reflect or resonate with you? Please sit with this question, and name them below.

Could the reason be a lack of assurance that God truly loves you? Write your thoughts below.

Could this be the key to the difference between Saul and David? Let's be honest, both men did their share of bad deeds. If you are unfamiliar with David's poor choices, just keep reading 2 Samuel! The difference between them wasn't their actions but their hearts. I do not believe that Saul ever truly understood the love of God because I'm not sure he ever understood his need for it. A love that casts out all fear. A love that can be trusted. A love that rebukes, forgives, and restores. A love that is enough. A love that is extravagant! But according to Psalm 103, David did.

Read Psalm 103:11-12, written by David. How do these verses express David's intimate knowledge of God's love?

I believe that from the beginning, Saul was chosen based on his outer appearance. There was not another like him in the land. The hopes of all Israel rested on him. If there was a man who could pull this job off, they thought it would be him. But wasn't that the point? There wasn't a man—any man—who could pull this job off. This was a lesson for the people as well as for Saul. Apart from God, this job was impossible. Ultimately, God was their king, and although they had a physical king, that would in no way diminish their need to trust God. King or no king, God was still in control.

The Israelites continually desired the blessings of God over the presence of God. Both sons in Luke 15 wanted the riches of their father over his presence. One tried to attain it through self-indulgence, the other through self-denial. The younger son finally realized that the inheritance *was* the father, who had been available all along. The elder brother attempted to use his obedience to manipulate and control the father.

God will not be controlled. Matthew 9:35-38 reminds us that God is the "Lord of the harvest." The harvest is the outcome. Therefore, God is in control of outcomes. We are not! We are the lords or managers of the seed. We sow and trust our Father for the outcome. We walk each step He lights before us, trusting Him for the destination.

What outcome are you working hard to control? How's that working out?

If you chose to stop controlling and start loving, what would that look like?

Check out the definition of *prodigal*: "spending money or using resources freely and recklessly; wastefully extravagant."[13] This word was used to describe the younger son, but could it also describe the father? The elder son thought so! In his "humble" opinion (see what I did there), this love party was reckless and wasteful, so the elder son tried leveraging his obedience to restrain the love and grace of the father. Impossible! He could not control the father's love and grace, but he could experience it. If only he would drop his pride and see his need. If only he would walk into the party.

It's scary to realize that we have based our lives on a lie, that is, that we have been operating like fearful slaves when all along we have been daughters. Love changes everything! Love turns duty to pleasure. Love turns fear to trust.

If only Saul had let go and "entered the party." If only Saul had taken a risk by betting on the reckless, extravagant love of God. Instead, it seems he lived his life to the tune of "I did it my way" and died to the rhythm of these lines from an Emily Dickinson poem:

The Ruin was from within
Oh cunning wreck that told no tale[14]

Scripture seems to suggest that Saul died with his "mask" still on, trying to appear strong on the outside while fear reigned on the inside.

Extra Insight

In biblical times, tearing one's garments, or tearing a slit in a piece of clothing, was a sign of grief and distress. Other actions associated with mourning included lying or sitting in silence, bowing one's head, fasting, and sprinkling one's head with dirt, dust, or ashes.[15]

As we conclude our study, let us join David in singing a lament to the family of Saul. Read 2 Samuel 1:17-27. What phrase is repeated three times in this lament?

If I were to name this lament, I would title it, "How the mighty have fallen," since David repeats these words three times. I believe each time they represent a new wave of emotion as his grief sinks deeper.

Starting with verse 19, list below all that David was grieving.

Verse 19:

Verse 23:

Verse 24:

Verse 26:

David began by feeling the overall devastating loss of the nation, and then with each cry of "how the mighty have fallen," he worked his way deeper into his own personal grief, ending with his greatest loss, that of his friend Jonathan.

How I can understand this lament! Grief takes time. Just when you think you are done, another wave hits. We must allow it to wash over us; that is the only way through.

After all that he had endured under the hand of Saul, why do you think David was able to write such a heartfelt lament for him?

Could it be because David was the "younger brother" in Luke 15:11-32? Write your thoughts about that below.

Like David, we must learn to lament our losses, trusting in God's love and provision and believing that His good plans will prevail. Remember, David began as an overlooked son in a shepherd's field but, soon after his anointing, began one massive victory tour. Yet when the tour came to an end, David experienced one loss after another. He lost his family, his home, his best friend, and his mentor Samuel. He experienced rejection, false accusation, and solitude. If anyone could write "Oh how the mighty have fallen" and truly understand the descent, it was David. For years he lived as a fugitive while holding on to a promise that seems like a mist. David was forced to live by faith looking forward while we have the scriptural hindsight to know that God *was* in control of David's life and destiny. David went on to become the reigning king of Israel and . . . Not only that, but God's own Son came through David's line!

Jesus is a different kind of "elder brother." Unlike the elder brother in the parable, He was willing to lay down not only all of His inheritance but also His life in order that what was lost could be found. He fully understood the love of the Father and could not wait for us to experience it! And He himself has sent us the invitation to the party. Have you accepted?

Come to the table
Come join the sinners who have been redeemed[16]

That, my friend, is where we find mercy and freedom. That is where we realize that to lose control—to surrender our lives to Jesus—is how we find our soul. And that is the greatest exchange we will ever make!

Prayer Prompt

What is keeping you from coming to the party and taking your seat at the table? Talk with God about anything that is holding you back. Are you living as a fearful slave or a beloved daughter? Ask God to help you receive and rest in His extravagant love! Tell God that you want to lose control and find your soul in Him.

To lose control— to surrender our lives to Jesus— is how we find our soul.

When _____ thoughts start making their rounds, it is easy to detour to the "land of settle."

Sometimes when we are exhausted from battles and plagued by loss, we _____.

The key is not in the chaos but in the _____ to it.

Even when everything seems out of control, God is at _____.

Even after the chaos of _____, _____ came. The stone was rolled away.

When you are in the abyss, it's easy to forget the Spirit of God is _____.

We may _____, but God doesn't.

Scriptures: 1 Samuel 27:1, John 4, 1 Samuel 28–30, Genesis 1:1

Video Viewer Guide Answers

Week 1
work / control
do / Jesus
insecurities
love cup
Feelings / slaves
equipped
His

Week 2
delays / detours
model / endorse
trust
Awareness
represent
Spirit / idol
love

Week 3
peace
captives free
restore
bring life
define / develop
lasting effect
Word

Week 4
anticipation / reality
perspective / sight
cloud / rain
face / bullies
equipped
armor

Week 5
question
sorrows / human
Nothing
mystery
race / weight
brokenness

Week 6
hopeless
withdraw
response
work
Friday / Sunday
hovering
settle

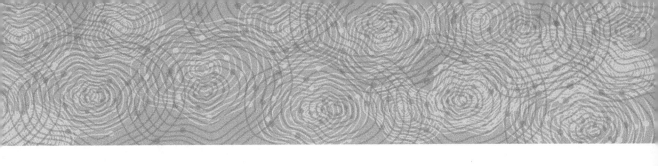

Notes

Biblical Background

1. "The Land: Geography and Climate," Israel Ministry of Foreign Affairs, http://www.israel.org/mfa/aboutisrael/land/pages/the%20land-%20geography%20and%20climate.aspx.
2. "Comparison of the Size of Israel vs. New Jersey," Information Regarding Israel's Security, http://iris.org.il/israel-and-new-jersey/.
3. "Ancient Jewish History: Via Maris," Jewish Virtual Library, https://www.jewishvirtuallibrary.org/via-maris.

Week 1

1. "1 Samuel 1," Benson Commentary, biblehub.com/commentaries/benson/1_samuel/1.htm.
2. Blue Letter Bible, s.v. "beliya`al," www.blueletterbible.org/lang/lexicon/lexicon.cfm?Strongs=H1100&t=NIV
3. Robert Rezeertko and Ian Young, *Historical Linguistics and Biblical Hebrew: Steps Toward an Integrated Approach* (Atlanta: SBL Press, 2014), 485.
4. Dictionary.com, s.v. "minister," www.dictionary.com/browse/minister.
5. Blue Letter Bible, s.v. "keheh," www.blueletterbible.org/lang/lexicon/lexicon.cfm?Strongs=H3544&t=KJV.
6. Blue Letter Bible, s.v. "kahah," www.blueletterbible.org/lang/lexicon/lexicon.cfm?Strongs=H3543&t=KJV.
7. GoodSeed, s.v., "lampstand," www.goodseed.com/menorah---lampstand.html.
8. GoodSeed, s.v., "table of showbread," www.goodseed.com/table-of-showbread.html.
9. GoodSeed, s.v., "alter of incense," https://www.goodseed.com/golden-altar-of-incense.html.
10. Blue Letter Bible, s.v, "yada'," www.blueletterbible.org/lang/lexicon/lexicon.cfm?Strongs=H3045&t=KJV.
11. Encyclopædia Britannica, s.v "Philistine," www.britannica.com/topic/philistine-people.
12. National Museum of History, s.v. "Shofar," https://americanhistory.si.edu/collections/search/object/nmah_1160973.
13. Theodore E. Schmauk, *Bible Geography for Schools* (Philadelphia: Board of Publication of the General Council of the Evangelical Lutheran Church in North America, 1899, 1906), 156.
14. Blue Letter Bible, s.v. "kabad," www.blueletterbible.org/lang/lexicon/lexicon.cfm?Strongs=H3513&t=KJV.
15. Bible Study Tools, s.v. "emerods," www.biblestudytools.com/dictionary/emerods.
16. Kristofor Husted, "Why Do Cows Moo? Here Are a Few Reasons," Harvest Public Media, www.harvestpublicmedia.org/post/why-do-cows-moo-here-are-few-reasons.
17. Menachem Posner, "Who Were the Levites?," Chabad.org, www.chabad.org/library/article_cdo/aid/4254752/jewish/Who-Were-the-Levites.htm.
18. Jamiseon, Fausset & Brown, "Commentary on 1 Samuel 6," Blue Letter Bible, www.blueletterbible.org/Comm/jfb/1Sa/1Sa_006.cfm?a=242019.
19. David Guzik, "Study Guide for 1 Samuel 6," Blue Letter Bible, www.blueletterbible.org/Comm/guzik_david/StudyGuide2017-1Sa/1Sa-6.cfm?a=242019.

20. "Acacia," Bible Plants, ODU Bible Plants Site, https://ww2.odu.edu/~lmusselm/plant/bible/acacia.php.
21. Casey Hofford, "Everything You Need to Know About Acacia Trees," Plantsnap, www.plantsnap.com/blog/everything-acacia-trees/.
22. Dr. J. Vernon McGee, "Chapter IX: The Ark of Gold and Wood: The Doctrine of Christology," Blue Letter Bible, https://www.blueletterbible.org/Comm/mcgee_j_vernon/eBooks/tabernacle/chapter-ix-the-ark-of-gold-and-wood.cfm.
23. Brennan Manning, *The Ragamuffin Gospel: Good News for the Bedraggled, Beat-Up, and Burnt Out* (Multnomah Press, 2005), 46.

Week 2

1.   Bible Hub, s.v. "Beth Kar," https://biblehub.com/hebrew/1033.htm.
2.   "Word Counts: How Many Times Does a Word Appear in the Bible?," Christian Bible Reference Site, https://www.christianbiblereference.org/faq_WordCount.htm.
3.   Joseph Benson, "Commentary on 1 Samuel 9:4," Study Light, https://www.studylight.org/commentaries/rbc/1-samuel-9.html.
4.   The Jewish Chronicle, s.v. "beged," https://www.thejc.com/judaism/jewish-words/beged-1.5785.
5.   John Gill, "Commentary on 1 Samuel 9:4," Study Light, https://www.studylight.org/commentaries/geb/1-samuel-9.html.
6.   Adam Clarke, "Commentary on 1 Samuel 9:4," Study Light, https://www.studylight.org/commentaries/acc/1-samuel-9.html.
7.   David Guzik, "Study Guide for 1 Samuel 9," Blue Letter Bible, https://www.blueletterbible.org/Comm/guzik_david/StudyGuide2017-1Sa/1Sa-9.cfm?a=245001.
8.   "What Was the Practice of Casting Lots?," Got Questions, https://www.gotquestions.org/casting-lots.html.
9.   "Ancient Jewish History: The Urim and Thummim," Jewish Virtual Library, https://www.jewishvirtuallibrary.org/the-urim-and-thummim.
10. Søren Kierkegaard, Journalen JJ:167 (1843), Søren Kierkegaards Skrifter, Søren Kierkegaard Research Center, Copenhagen, 1997--, volume 18, page 306, http://homepage.math.uiowa.edu/~jorgen/kierkegaardquotesource.html.
11. Brené Brown, "Why Your Critics Aren't the Ones Who Count," 99U, December 4, 2013, YouTube video, 8:53, https://www.youtube.com/watch?v=8-JXOnFOXQk.
12. Holman Bible Dictionary, s.v. "Jabesh-gilead," Study Light, https://www.studylight.org/dictionaries/hbd/j/jabesh-gilead.html.
13. Bible Tools, s.v. "Nahash," https://www.bibletools.org/index.cfm/fuseaction/Lexicon.show/ID/H5176/Nachash.htm.
14. Blue Letter Bible, s.v. "'aph," https://www.blueletterbible.org/lang/lexicon/lexicon.cfm?t=kjv&strongs=h639.
15. Strong's Concordance, s.v. "zelos," Bible Hub, https://biblehub.com/greek/2205.htm.
16. John Parkhurst, *A Greek and English Lexicon to the New Testament* (Arkose Press, 2015), 248.

Week 3

1.   Jamiseon, Fausset & Brown, "Commentary on 1 Samuel 12," Blue Letter Bible, https://www.blueletterbible.org/Comm/jfb/1Sa/1Sa_012.cfm?a=248001.

2.   Jacob Isaacs, "War with the Philistines," Chabad.org, https://www.chabad.org/library/article_cdo/aid/464038/jewish/War-with-the-Philistines.htm.

3.   "An Introduction to the Book of Second Samuel," Bible.org, https://bible.org/article/introduction-book-second-samuel.

4.   Lyman Coleman, An Historical Text Book and Atlas of Biblical Geography (Virginia: Claxton, Remsen & Haffelfinger, 1854), 109. Digitized 2010.

5.   Phil Hopersberger, "The Philistines," Experience the Land of the Bible, http://www.land-of-the-bible.com/The_Philistines.

6.   Robert D. Bergen, 1, 2 Samuel: An Exegetical and Theological Exposition of Holy Scripture, The New American Commentary (Nashville: Holman Reference, 1996), 149.

7.   David Guzik, "1 Samuel 13–Saul's Disobedience," Enduring Word, https://enduringword.com/bible-commentary/1-samuel-13/.

8.   Torrey's Topical Textbook, s.v. "Ark of the Covenant," Study Light, https://www.studylight.org/concordances/ttt/a/ark-of-the-covenant.html.

9.   Blue Letter Bible, s.v. "Yehownathan," https://www.blueletterbible.org/lang/lexicon/lexicon.cfm?Strongs=H3083&t=NIV.

10.   Blue Letter Bible, s.v. "bow'," https://www.blueletterbible.org/lang/lexicon/lexicon.cfm?Strongs=H935&t=KJV.

11.   David Guzik, "Study Guide for 1 Samuel 15," Blue Letter Bible, https://www.blueletterbible.org/Comm/guzik_david/StudyGuide2017-1Sa/1Sa-15.cfm?a=251001.

12.   Don Stewart, "How Does God's Dealings with Nations Demonstrate His Existence?," Blue Letter Bible, https://www.blueletterbible.org/faq/don_stewart/don_stewart_374.cfm.

13.   Blue Letter Bible, s.v. "machah," https://www.blueletterbible.org/lang/lexicon/lexicon.cfm?Strongs=H4229&t=KJV.

14.   Dr. J. Vernon McGee, "Comments for 1 Samuel," Blue Letter Bible, https://www.blueletterbible.org/Comm/mcgee_j_vernon/notes-outlines/1samuel/1samuel-comments.cfm?a=251011.

15.   David Guzik, "Study Guide for 1 Samuel 15," Blue Letter Bible, https://www.blueletterbible.org/Comm/guzik_david/StudyGuide2017-1Sa/1Sa-15.cfm?a=251011.

16.   David Guzik, "Study Guide for 1 Samuel 15," Blue Letter Bible, https://www.blueletterbible.org/Comm/guzik_david/StudyGuide2017-1Sa/1Sa-15.cfm.

17.   Friedrich Nietzsche, Beyond Good and Evil (United States: 1st World Library, 2004), 88. (Original publication date in 1886).

18.   J.D. Greer and Heath A. Thomas, Exalting Jesus in 1 & 2 Samuel (United States: B&H Publishing Group, 2016), 122–123.

Week 4

1.   Strong's Concordance, s.v. "ba'ath," Blue Letter Bible, https://www.blueletterbible.org/lang/lexicon/lexicon.cfm?Strongs=H1204&t=KJV.

2.   The Cambridge Bible for Schools and Colleges, "1 Samuel 16," Benson Commentary on the Old and New Testaments, Bible Hub, https://biblehub.com/commentaries/cambridge/1_samuel/16.htm.

3.   David Guzik, "1 Samuel 16," Bible Hub, https://biblehub.com/commentaries/benson/1_samuel/16.htm.

4. Strong's Concordance, s.v. "ravach," Blue Letter Bible, https://www.blueletterbible.org/lang/lexicon/lexicon.cfm?t=kjv&strongs=h7304.
5. Rick Nauert, PhD, "Music Sooths Anxiety, Reduces Pain," Psych Central, https://psychcentral.com/news/2018/12/23/music-soothes-anxiety-reduces-pain/32952.html.
6. Emily Saarman, "Feeling the Beat: Symposium Explores the Therapeutic Effects of Rhythmic Music," Stanford News, https://news.stanford.edu/news/2006/may31/brainwave-053106.html.
7. Encyclopædia Britannica, s.v. "kinnor," https://www.britannica.com/art/kinnor.
8. Ray Vander Laan, "Via Maris," That the World May Know, https://www.thattheworldmayknow.com/via-maris.
9. Dr. Ralph F. Wilson, "David and Goliath: Bold Faith," Jesus Walk, http://www.jesuswalk.com/david/02_david_goliath.htm#_ftn47.
10. Matthew George Easton, "Easton's Bible Dictionary," s.v. "champion," Bible Study Tools, https://www.biblestudytools.com/dictionary/champion/.
11. Online Etymology Dictionary, s.v. "mano a mano," https://www.etymonline.com/word/mano%20a%20mano.
12. Theodore Roosevelt, "Citizenship in a Republic" (speech, Sorbonne, Paris, April 23, 1910), in The Works of Theodore Roosevelt, Vol. XIII (Illinois: University of Illinois at Urbana-Champaign, 1896) 506-529.
13. "The Toughest Man Alive: Interview with Retired Navy Seal David Goggins," Connecting Vets, https://connectingvets.radio.com/articles/david-goggins-retired-navy-seal-toughest-man-alive.
14. David Goggins, "What do you say to yourself when life is kicking your a..?," Facebook, February 24, 2017, https://www.facebook.com/iamdavidgoggins/posts/587477391463624:0.
15. "New Study Suggests We Remember the Bad Times Better Than the Good," Association for Psychological Science, https://www.psychologicalscience.org/news/releases/new-study-suggests-we-remember-the-bad-times-better-than-the-good.html.
16. Eric Lyons, "Did Saul Know David Prior to Goliath's Death?," Apologetics Press, https://www.apologeticspress.org/apcontent.aspx?category=6&article=807.
17. Charles R. Swindoll, David: A Man of Passion and Destiny (Nashville: Thomas Nelson, 1997), 52.
18. Jonathan Sacks, "The Bond of Loyalty and Love," Covenant and Conversation, http://rabbisacks.org/bond-loyalty-love-yitro-5778/.
19. Precept Austin, s.v. "beriyth," https://www.preceptaustin.org/covenant_definition.
20. David Guzik, "Study Guide for Genesis 15," Blue Letter Bible, https://www.blueletterbible.org/Comm/guzik_david/StudyGuide2017-Gen/Gen-15.cfm?a=15001.
21. Scott Slayton, "3 Truths About Genuine Friendship We Can Learn from David and Jonathan," Crosswalk, https://www.crosswalk.com/faith/spiritual-life/3-truths-about-genuine-friendship-we-can-learn-from-david-and-jonathan.html.
22. Amy Cummins, "Finding Happiness in Others' Success," Grit and Virtue, https://gritandvirtue.com/finding-happiness-in-others-success/.
23. Merriam Webster, s.v. "envy," https://www.merriam-webster.com/dictionary/envy.
24. Ed Mylett, host, "My #1 Key to Happiness," The Ed Mylett Show (podcast), June 4, 2019, https://edmylett.libsyn.com/my-1-key-to-happiness.
25. Mylett, "My #1 Key to Happiness."

26. Melissa Crutchfield, "Who Am I? A New Way to Define Identity," Cru, https://www.cru.org/us/en/blog/life-and-relationships/identity/who-am-i-a-new-way-to-define-identity.html.
27. "Brené Brown on the Difference Between Guilt and Shame," Farnam Street Media Inc., https://fs.blog/2014/10/brene-brown-guilt-shame/.
28. Darlene Lancer, "How Insecurity Leads to Envy, Jealousy, and Shame," PsychCentral, https://psychcentral.com/lib/envy-jealousy-and-shame/.
29. Strong's Concordance, s.v. "prophesy," Blue Letter Bible, https://www.blueletterbible.org/lang/lexicon/lexicon.cfm?Strongs=H5012&t=KJV.
30. Smith's Bible Dictionary, s.v. "prophet," Blue Letter Bible, https://www.blueletterbible.org/search/dictionary/viewtopic.cfm?topic=BT0003456.
31. "What Was the School of Prophets?" Got Questions, https://www.gotquestions.org/school-of-prophets.html.
32. Strong's Concordance, s.v. "panah," Bible Hub, https://biblehub.com/hebrew/6440.htm.
33. David Guzik, "Study Guide for 1 Samuel 21," Blue Letter Bible, https://www.blueletterbible.org/Comm/guzik_david/StudyGuide2017-1Sa/1Sa-21.cfm?a=257001.

Week 5

1. Amanda Borschel-Dan, "Colossal Ancient Structures Found at Gath May Explain Origin of Story of Goliath," The Times of Israel, July 26, 2019, https://www.timesofisrael.com/colossal-ancient-structures-found-at-gath-may-explain-origin-of-story-of-goliath/.
2. David Guzik, "Study Guide for 1 Samuel 21," Bible Hub, https://www.blueletterbible.org/Comm/guzik_david/StudyGuide2017-1Sa/1Sa-21.cfm?a=257012.
3. Charles Swindoll, David: A Man of Passion and Destiny (Thomas Nelson: 1997), 73.
4. Strong's Concordance, s.v. "surrounded," Bible Hub, https://biblehub.com/greek/4029.htm.
5. Steph Redhead. Instagram post, May 7, 2015, https://www.instagram.com/p/2ZFctzBT21/.
6. Baltasar Gracian, The Art of Worldly Wisdom, trans. Christopher Maurer (New York: Doubleday, 1992), 2.
7. Nichole Nordeman, vocalist, "Sound of Surviving," by Tommee Profitt and Nichole Nordeman, track 9 on Every Mile Mattered, Sparrow Records, 2017; Copyright © 2017 Birdwing Music (ASCAP) Tommee Profitt Songs (ASCAP) Birdboy Songs (ASCAP) Capitol CMB Genesis (ASCAP) (adm. at CapitolCMGPublishing.com).
8. David Guzik, "Study Guide for 1 Samuel 23," Blue Letter Bible, https://www.blueletterbible.org/Comm/guzik_david/StudyGuide2017-1Sa/1Sa-23.cfm?a=259001.
9. "En Gedi," BiblePlaces.com, https://www.bibleplaces.com/engedi/.
10. "En Gedi," Jewish Virtual Library, https://www.jewishvirtuallibrary.org/vie-ein-gedi.
11. John Gill, "Commentary on Psalm 63:4," The New John Gill Exposition of the Entire Bible, https://www.studylight.org/commentaries/geb/psalms-63.html.
12. James K. Summers and Deborah N. Vivian, "Ecotherapy—A Forgotten Ecosystem Service: A Review," Frontiers in Psychology 9 (2018): 1389, https://www.ncbi.nlm.nih.gov/pmc/articles/PMC6085576/.
13. "Sour Mood Getting You Down? Get Back to Nature," Harvard Men's Health Watch, July 2018, https://www.health.harvard.edu/mind-and-mood/sour-mood-getting-you-down-get-back-to-nature.
14. "Sour Mood," Harvard Men's Health Watch.

15. Etz Hayim Study Companion, eds. Jacob Blumenthal and Janet L. Liss (New York: The Jewish Publication Society, The Rabbinical Assembly, 2005), 266.
16. "Death & Bereavement in Judaism: Ancient Burial Practices," Jewish Virtual Library, https://www.jewishvirtuallibrary.org/ancient-burial-practices.
17. Abarim Publications, s.v. "Abigail," https://www.abarim-publications.com/Meaning/Abigail.html#.XvJFmFB7nJw.
18. Quick Reference Dictionary, s.v. "Sheep-Shearing," https://www.biblestudytools.com/dictionary/sheep-shearing/.
19. Swindoll, David, 95.
20. James Moyer, "The Bible: Weapons and Warfare in Ancient Israel," Grace Communion International, https://www.gci.org/articles/weapons-and-warfare-in-ancient-israel/.

Week 6

1. Behind the Name, s.v. "Reuben," https://www.behindthename.com/name/reuben.
2. Behind the Name, s.v. "Simeon," http://www.behindthename.com/name/simeon.
3. Behind the Name, s.v. "Levi," https://www.behindthename.com/name/levi.
4. Baruch Altein, "Who Were Amalek and the Amalekites?," Chabad-Lubavitch Media Center, https://www.chabad.org/library/article_cdo/aid/3942715/jewish/Who-Were-Amalek-and-the-Amalekites.htm.
5. "The Ark of the Covenant Is Captured at Aphek," The Bible Journey, https://www.thebiblejourney.org/biblejourney2/29-the-journeys-of-ruth-and-samuel/the-ark-of-the-covenant-is-captured-at-aphek/.
6. Robert Evans Wilson Jr., "Fear vs. Power," Psychology Today, https://www.psychologytoday.com/us/blog/the-main-ingredient/201303/fear-vs-power.
7. Easton's Bible Dictionary, s.v. "familiar spirit," Blue Letter Bible, https://www.blueletterbible.org/search/dictionary/viewtopic.cfm?topic=ET0001307.
8. Don Stewart," Did the Spirit of Samuel Communicate to Saul at En Dor?," https://www.blueletterbible.org/faq/don_stewart/don_stewart_121.cfm.
9. "Who Was Asherah/Ashtoreth?," Got Questions Ministries, https://www.gotquestions.org/who-Asherah.html.
10. Wisdom for the Soul, ed. Larry Chang (Washington, D.C.: Gnosophia Publishers, 2006), 304.
11. Timothy Keller, The Prodigal God: Recovering the Heart of the Christian Faith (New York: Dutton, 2008), 58.
12. Keller, The Prodigal God, 63–64.
13. Lexico, s.v. "prodigal," https://www.lexico.com/definition/prodigal.
14. The Poems of Emily Dickinson, ed. Thomas H. Johnson (Cambridge, MA: The Belknap Press of Harvard University Press, 1979), 788.
15. Encyclopedia of the Bible, s.v. "mourning," Bible Gateway, https://www.biblegateway.com/resources/encyclopedia-of-the-bible/Mourning.
16. Sidewalk Prophets, "Come to the Table," by Ben McDonald, Dave Frey, Ben Glover, track 8 on Something Different, Fervent / Word, 2015; Copyright © 2015. 9t One Songs (Admin. by Capitol CMG Publishing) / Ariose Music (Admin. by Capitol CMG Publishing) / Pencil Prophet Publishing (Admin. by CURB | Word Music Publishing) / Run Run Milo (Admin. by CURB | Word Music Publishing) / Curb Dayspring Music (Admin. by Warner-Tamerlane Publishing Corp.).

CPSIA information can be obtained
at www.ICGtesting.com
Printed in the USA
LVHW022051071120
670999LV00001B/1